OPPOSING VIEWPOINTS® SERIES

I Refugees

DISCARD

Other Books of Related Interest:

Opposing Viewpoints Series

Human Rights

Immigration

Social Justice

Tibet

The United Nations

Current Controversies Series

Afghanistan

Darfur

Immigration

At Issue Series

How Should the U.S. Proceed in Afghanistan?

Should the U.S. Close Its Borders?

What Is the Impact of Immigration?

"Congress shall make no law ... abridging the freedom of speech, or of the press."

First Amendment to the U.S. Constitution

The basic foundation of our democracy is the First Amendment guarantee of freedom of expression. The Opposing Viewpoints Series is dedicated to the concept of this basic freedom and the idea that it is more important to practice it than to enshrine it.

Refugees

Margaret Haerens, Book Editor

GREENHAVEN PRESS
A part of Gale, Cengage Learning

GALE
CENGAGE Learning™

Detroit • New York • San Francisco • New Haven, Conn • Waterville, Maine • London

GALE
CENGAGE Learning™

Christine Nasso, *Publisher*
Elizabeth Des Chenes, *Managing Editor*

© 2010 Greenhaven Press, a part of Gale, Cengage Learning.

Gale and Greenhaven Press are registered trademarks used herein under license.

For more information, contact:
Greenhaven Press
27500 Drake Rd.
Farmington Hills, MI 48331-3535
Or you can visit our Internet site at gale.cengage.com

For product information and technology assistance, contact us at

Gale Customer Support, 1-800-877-4253
For permission to use material from this text or product, submit all requests online at www.cengage.com/permissions

Further permissions questions can be emailed to permissionrequest@cengage.com

Articles in Greenhaven Press anthologies are often edited for length to meet page require-ments. In addition, original titles of these works are changed to clearly present the main thesis and to explicitly indicate the author's opinion. Every effort is made to ensure that Greenhaven Press accurately reflects the original intent of the authors. Every effort has been made to trace the owners of copyrighted material.

Cover image copyright Mehmet Yunns, 2009. Used under license from Shutterstock.com.

LIBRARY OF CONGRESS CATALOGING-IN-PUBLICATION DATA

Refugees / Margaret Haerens, book editor.
    p. cm. -- (Opposing viewpoints)
    Includes bibliographical references and index.
    978-0-7377-4224-4 (hbk.)
    978-0-7377-4225-1 (pbk.)
    1. Refugees--Juvenile literature. 2. Refugees--Government policy--Juvenile lit-erature. I. Haerens, Margaret.
    JV6346.R4R424 2009
    362.87--dc22
                                                                2009023049

Printed in the United States of America
1 2 3 4 5 6 7 13 12 11 10 09

Contents

Why Consider Opposing Viewpoints?   11

Introduction   14

Chapter 1: How Serious Is the Refugee Problem?

Chapter Preface   19

1. There Is a Serious Refugee Problem Worldwide   21
   Lavinia Limón

2. The Boundaries Between the Refugee and   25
   Migrant Problems Are Often Blurred
   José Riera

3. Climate Refugees Are a Growing Problem   31
   Teresita Perez

4. The Climate Refugee Problem Is Exaggerated   36
   Mike Hulme

5. The Iraqi Refugee Problem Is a Crisis   42
   Stephen Glain

6. The Iraqi Refugee Problem Has   48
   Been Exaggerated
   Amir Taheri

7. Refugees Are a Significant National   55
   Security Threat
   Thomas Allen

8. Refugees Are Not a Serious National   60
   Security Threat
   Anna Husarska

Periodical Bibliography   65

Chapter 2: Who Is Responsible for Aiding Refugees?

Chapter Preface   67

1. The International Community Should   **69**
   Help Alleviate the Refugee Problem
   António Guterres

2. National Governments Have an Obligation   **75**
   to Refugees
   David Anthony Denny

3. Non-Governmental Organizations Have   **80**
   an Obligation to Refugees
   Ed Schenkenberg van Mierop

4. The UN High Commissioner for Refugees   **87**
   Should Be Responsible for the Refugee Problem
   Thomas Albrecht

5. The UN High Commissioner for   **97**
   Refugees Should Have Less Responsibility
   for the Refugee Problem
   Mauro De Lorenzo

6. The United States Should Do More   **104**
   for Iraqi Refugees
   Brian Katulis and Peter Juul

7. The United States Has Done a Great Deal   **109**
   for Iraqi Refugees
   Ellen R. Sauerbrey

Periodical Bibliography   **116**

Chapter 3: What U.S. Policies Can Help Alleviate the Refugee Problem?

Chapter Preface   **118**

1. U.S. Immigration Policy Is Working Correctly   **120**
   Ellen R. Sauerbrey

2. U.S. Immigration Policy Has Made It Too   **127**
   Difficult for Refugees to Enter the Country
   Kerry Howley

3. The United States Should Limit the Number   **131**
of Refugees Entering the Country
Thomas Allen

4. Increasing Development Assistance Can   **138**
Help Solve the Refugee Problem
Merrill Smith

5. The United States Should Help Refugees   **147**
Wrongly Accused of Supporting Terrorists
Human Rights First

6. The United States Should Be Cautious Admitting   **153**
Refugees Accused of Supporting Terrorists
Paul Rosenzweig

Periodical Bibliography   **163**

Chapter 4: What International Policies Can Alleviate the Refugee Problem?

Chapter Preface   **165**

1. Safe Repatriation Can Alleviate   **167**
the Refugee Problem
The Economist

2. Resettlement Can Help Solve   **174**
the Refugee Problem
United Nations High Commissioner for Refugees

3. Integration Can Alleviate   **180**
the Refugee Problem
Sarah J. Feldman

4. Supporting Refugee Rights Can   **185**
Help the Refugee Problem
Barbara Harrell-Bond and Mike Kagan

5. Refugee Camps Are a Necessary Evil   **197**
Voice of America

Periodical Bibliography   **202**

For Further Discussion   203
Organizations to Contact   206
Bibliography of Books   212
Index   216

Why Consider Opposing Viewpoints?

"The only way in which a human being can make some approach to knowing the whole of a subject is by hearing what can be said about it by persons of every variety of opinion and studying all modes in which it can be looked at by every character of mind. No wise man ever acquired his wisdom in any mode but this."

John Stuart Mill

In our media-intensive culture it is not difficult to find differing opinions. Thousands of newspapers and magazines and dozens of radio and television talk shows resound with differing points of view. The difficulty lies in deciding which opinion to agree with and which "experts" seem the most credible. The more inundated we become with differing opinions and claims, the more essential it is to hone critical reading and thinking skills to evaluate these ideas. Opposing Viewpoints books address this problem directly by presenting stimulating debates that can be used to enhance and teach these skills. The varied opinions contained in each book examine many different aspects of a single issue. While examining these conveniently edited opposing views, readers can develop critical thinking skills such as the ability to compare and contrast authors' credibility, facts, argumentation styles, use of persuasive techniques, and other stylistic tools. In short, the Opposing Viewpoints Series is an ideal way to attain the higher-level thinking and reading skills so essential in a culture of diverse and contradictory opinions.

In addition to providing a tool for critical thinking, Opposing Viewpoints books challenge readers to question their own strongly held opinions and assumptions. Most people form their opinions on the basis of upbringing, peer pressure, and personal, cultural, or professional bias. By reading carefully balanced opposing views, readers must directly confront new ideas as well as the opinions of those with whom they disagree. This is not to simplistically argue that everyone who reads opposing views will—or should—change his or her opinion. Instead, the series enhances readers' understanding of their own views by encouraging confrontation with opposing ideas. Careful examination of others' views can lead to the readers' understanding of the logical inconsistencies in their own opinions, perspective on why they hold an opinion, and the consideration of the possibility that their opinion requires further evaluation.

Evaluating Other Opinions

To ensure that this type of examination occurs, Opposing Viewpoints books present all types of opinions. Prominent spokespeople on different sides of each issue as well as well-known professionals from many disciplines challenge the reader. An additional goal of the series is to provide a forum for other, less known, or even unpopular viewpoints. The opinion of an ordinary person who has had to make the decision to cut off life support from a terminally ill relative, for example, may be just as valuable and provide just as much insight as a medical ethicist's professional opinion. The editors have two additional purposes in including these less known views. One, the editors encourage readers to respect others' opinions—even when not enhanced by professional credibility. It is only by reading or listening to and objectively evaluating others' ideas that one can determine whether they are worthy of consideration. Two, the inclusion of such viewpoints encourages the important critical thinking skill of objectively evaluating an author's credentials and bias. This evaluation will illuminate an author's reasons for taking a particular stance on an issue and will aid in readers' evaluation of the author's ideas.

It is our hope that these books will give readers a deeper understanding of the issues debated and an appreciation of the complexity of even seemingly simple issues when good and honest people disagree. This awareness is particularly important in a democratic society such as ours in which people enter into public debate to determine the common good. Those with whom one disagrees should not be regarded as enemies but rather as people whose views deserve careful examination and may shed light on one's own.

Thomas Jefferson once said that "difference of opinion leads to inquiry, and inquiry to truth." Jefferson, a broadly educated man, argued that "if a nation expects to be ignorant and free . . . it expects what never was and never will be." As individuals and as a nation, it is imperative that we consider the opinions of others and examine them with skill and discernment. The Opposing Viewpoints Series is intended to help readers achieve this goal.

David L. Bender and Bruno Leone,
Founders

Introduction

"So often the world sits idly by, watching ethnic conflicts flare up, as if these were mere entertainment rather than human beings whose lives are being destroyed. Shouldn't the existence of even one single refugee be a cause for alarm throughout the world?"

—Urkhan Alakbarov,
geneticist in an interview
with Azerbaijan International

In 2003, violence erupted in the Darfur region of Sudan, a large country located in northeastern Africa. Claiming that Darfur was being neglected by the government and that black Africans were being marginalized by ethnic Arab groups, rebels attacked government targets located in Darfur, the western region of the country. The government quickly retaliated by forming militia groups of its own, perhaps the most brutal of which is known as the Janjawid. The resulting conflict precipitated one of the worst humanitarian crises of modern times.

As a result of the fighting between the rebels and government-backed militia groups, it has been estimated that more than three hundred thousand Sudanese have been killed. Horrible atrocities have been committed against women and children; there have been numerous credible reports that the Janjawid has been perpetrating raids, bombings, and destructive attacks on villages, killing civilians based on ethnicity, raping women, and taking land and herds of livestock. So many people have been killed that on September 4, 2004, U.S. Secretary of State Colin Powell deemed the Darfur conflict an ongoing genocide.

Even after the Darfur Peace Agreement was signed in 2006, the fighting, raping, and killing continued. The conflict has spilled over into the neighboring country of Chad, which declared a state of war against the Sudan in 2005, citing raids and violence committed by Sudan-backed militia groups as the reason. A peace agreement between Chad and the Sudan was signed in 2007, but not before a number of raids and attacks killed and displaced thousands of citizens from the border region between the two countries.

The six-year conflict raging in the Darfur region has led to the internal displacement of more than 2.5 million people, most of them very poor black Africans that had been scraping out a living farming in small villages. These refugees have been forced into large displacement camps near the border with Chad, which has taken in another estimated two hundred and fifty thousand Sudanese refugees. The spread of the conflict into Chad has also uprooted over one hundred and seventy thousand Chadians who remain vulnerable to attacks by armed groups.

Instead of finding safety in refugee camps, however, refugees are often attacked by the marauding bands of Janjawid and other government-backed militia groups. Women are still being raped; people are still being killed; and the meager food and goods the refugees can get are being stolen. One of the central problems in Darfur and Chad is security, which has largely failed to protect refugees. Since most of the refugees are internally displaced persons (IDPs), or refugees that stay within the boundaries of their country of origin, they are still vulnerable to the ethnic conflict that rages outside of the camps. With a government unwilling or unable to provide protection from roving bands of violent militias, the Sudanese refugees are never truly safe.

International organizations and non-governmental organizations (NGOs) determined to provide humanitarian help for the displaced in the Darfur region have also been subjected to violence. Recent estimates have placed the number of aid workers in the Darfur region around fourteen thousand, all of them mobilized to address the serious and complex crisis facing the people of Darfur. Numerous aid workers have been raped, attacked, and murdered, and humanitarian supplies have been hijacked and stolen from the very people who need them the most. Furthermore, the United Nations (UN) peacekeeping mission authorized to implement the Darfur Peace Agreement, UNAMID, lacks adequate resources and troops.

Many Sudanese refugees who manage to escape to Chad are living in twelve huge refugee camps run by the United Nations High Commissioner for Refugees (UNHCR), where they receive shelter, food, education, and health care. The government of Chad has made a commitment not to return Sudanese refugees to their home country, and has honored that commitment. Due to the lack of national refugee policy within Chad, however, the refugees may languish in camps with no long-term solutions in sight. Even in Chad, however, in refugee camps run by UNHCR, the security of refugees is not assured. Many of the refugee camps in Chad that house Sudanese refugees have also been attacked by armed groups.

Certainly the issues faced by the refugees in Darfur and Chad are extreme, but in a sense they reveal the larger problems that national governments, international organizations, and non-governmental organizations concerned with the refugee crisis are faced with on a constant basis. Without the security of the refugees assured, and without basic services like shelter, food, and education, refugees will face long odds to survive. Without a concerted effort from governmental and humanitarian institutions, refugees will languish for years in refugee camps or migrate from place to place, without the chance to return home, resettle in a different country, or integrate locally. They will be deprived of the opportunity for personal and economic development and the chance for a safe, secure existence.

The authors of the viewpoints presented in *Opposing View-points: Refugees* discuss many challenges faced in alleviating the refugee crisis in the following chapters: "How Serious Is the Refugee Problem?" "Who Is Responsible for Aiding Refugees?" "What U.S. Policies Can Help Alleviate the Refugee Problem?" and "What International Policies Can Help Alleviate the Refugee Problem?" The information provided in this volume will provide insight into why the refugee crisis is such a severe global problem and what the worldwide community is doing to alleviate it.

OPPOSING VIEWPOINTS® SERIES

CHAPTER 1

How Serious Is the Refugee Problem?

Chapter Preface

Experts provide a number of reasons for the refugee problem. Perhaps the leading cause is the widespread economic, physical, and social devastation of armed conflict. When civil wars or insurgencies break out in a region, it is usually the native people who are affected the most. Forcibly displaced and unable to return to their homes, they often must leave their homeland to find safety. War and conflict also result in food scarcity; when agricultural production is disturbed, there is not enough food for the local population. If they can, those afflicted leave in search of food. Oppression is another reason residents leave their homes. When a government selectively oppresses a group of people for political, religious, or cultural reasons, the oppressed often migrate to find security, tolerance, and opportunity in other lands. In recent years, scholars have begun to note another troubling trend: climate refugees.

For the tiny South Pacific island nation of Tuvalu, the prospect of its entire population of eleven thousand people becoming climate refugees is very real. With the entire nation only fifteen feet above sea level at its highest, the rising ocean levels in recent years threaten to engulf the nine slender islands and atolls that comprise the country. Scientists believe that Tuvalu could be the first casualty of global warming; it is predicted that the entire nation could be underwater completely by the year 2050. Although some critics argue that Tuvalu's problems are actually caused by overpopulation and severe pollution, most scientists agree that Tuvalu faces a dire future, with its citizens eventually having to leave the doomed island nation.

If the forecasts of the effects of climate change are correct, many nations will be facing the harsh consequences of global warming in the future. In a number of areas, land once fertile and green will become barren; animals once abundant for hunting and eating will slowly disappear; and water will become scarce. Local populations will become climate refugees, forced to leave their homeland in order to find food. The climate refugee problem is a growing one, dependent on the progression and intensity of effects of climate change in the upcoming years.

The viewpoints collected in the following chapter examine the severity of the refugee crisis, focusing on the Iraq war and climate refugees. Although no one denies that there is a refugee problem, some commentators argue that the situation is exaggerated; some deny that global warming exists and, therefore, dismiss the notion of climate refugees; and still others reject the idea that refugees are national security threats.

"As history has shown us time and again, today's host may be tomorrow's refugee. . . . We ought to treat refugees as we ourselves would want to be treated."

There Is a Serious Refugee Problem Worldwide

Lavinia Limón

Lavinia Limón is president of the U.S. Committee for Refugees and Immigrants (USCRI). She also served as the director of the Office of Refugee Resettlement at the Department of Health and Human Services. In the following essay, Limón surveys the scope of the refugee crisis, outlining the reasons both poor and wealthy countries mistreat or reject refugees who need their help.

As you read, consider the following questions:

1. According to the *World Refugee Survey*, what was the total number of refugees in the world in 2007?

2. Why do countries adopt refugee policies that are illegal, immoral, and ineffective, according to the author?

3. What does the report cite as the largest refugee crisis of 2007?

Lavinia Limón, *World Refugee Survey 2008*, Arlington, VA: U.S. Committee of Refugees and Immigrants, 2008. © 2008 USCRI. Reproduced by permission.

Which is worse—turning refugees to face further away persecution, violence, and possibly death or letting them enter a country and subjecting them to decades of deprivation and stultifying limbo? We could not decide either so we included both types of behavior in our Worst Places for Refugees list. In either case, countries across the globe are flouting international law and violating refugees' rights.

In 2007, we report that the total number of refugees in the world has increased to more than 14 million. Clearly, their mistreatment has not dissuaded refugees from fleeing horrors unimaginable to most of us. So why do countries adopt policies that are illegal, immoral, and ineffective? Perhaps their real purpose is to demonstrate that they will always treat refugees worse than their own people. Perhaps politicians and policy makers believe that their own hold on power will be more secure if their own population feels some privilege compared to refugees.

It is typically not productive to speculate about someone's motives so the [*World Refugee*] *Survey* simply lays out the facts of refugees' plight and the facts are appalling.

The mistreatment of refugees is not limited to poor countries or undemocratic regimes. Wealthy industrial nations utilize policies designed to limit the number of refugees that enter their territory, explaining that they have limited resources, that refugees are unable to integrate, or that some other country had primary responsibility. Other countries claim national security reasons, ethnic and/or religious conflict, or a lack of tolerance from their own citizens. Clearly, some nations do not have the resources to care for refugees and must rely upon international assistance. Too often, this leads governments and international agencies to establish and maintain refugee camps that curtail refugees' freedom and self-reliance. No matter the rationale the result is the same—refugees are denied their rights under international law.

Refugees and Asylum Seekers Worldwide, 2007

AFRICA	TOTAL 2,799,500
AMERICAS AND THE CARIBBEAN	TOTAL 787,800
EUROPE	TOTAL 527,900
MIDDLE EAST AND NORTH AFRICA	TOTAL 6,380,200
EAST ASIA AND THE PACIFIC	TOTAL 934,700
SOUTH AND CENTRAL ASIA	TOTAL 2,617,200

This table reflects the total number of people seeking refuge and asylum in various regions of the world.

World Refugee Survey,
"Refugees and Asylum Seekers Worldwide," 2008.

The 2007 Crisis

The largest refugee crisis of 2007 is the exodus of Iraqi refugees from the violence and instability of their homeland. To date, over 2 million refugees are scattered throughout Syria, Jordan, Lebanon, Egypt, Turkey, and many other countries in the region and beyond. Neither the Iraqi government nor the countries that comprise the coalition forces in Iraq have taken responsibility for the well-being of these refugees. While the [George W.] Bush Administration and the United Kingdom are busy trying to win the war, they have provided no leadership toward ensuring the rights and well-being of the victims of this war. Europe, which for the most part warned of the dire humanitarian consequences of the war, has also done nothing to help the people they were so concerned about. Ironically, most of the refugees have found relative safety in Syria, a rogue nation according to this Administration, and Jordan, one of the United States' closest allies in the region. Of course, this is largely an accident of geography, but it also

23

demonstrates that adoption of Western values or democracy does not determine the treatment of refugees.

Our analysis indicates that the treatment of refugees is usually based on geopolitical concerns and, possibly more importantly, on the perceived kinship between the refugees and the host communities. When refugees and their hosts look the same, speak the same language, share the same religion or common cultural heritage, the hosts treat them more humanely and allow them to exercise more of their rights. When the refugees are historical enemies, have different racial characteristics, worship a different God, or come from very far away, the treatment becomes less and less humane. Perhaps this was understandable in years past, when foreigners were unusual. In today's shrinking world, where our very survival is dependent on our recognition of our common humanity, this behavior is anachronistic and unacceptable. As history has shown us time and again, today's host may be tomorrow's refugee. There is only one lesson to be taken from this—we ought to treat refugees as we ourselves would want to be treated.

| *"Refugee and migratory movements intersect in a number of different ways."*

The Boundaries Between the Refugee and Migrant Problems Are Often Blurred

José Riera

José Riera is senior policy advisor in the Policy Development and Evaluation Service at the Office of the United Nations High Commissioner for Refugees (UNHCR). In the following essay, Riera argues that in recent years the line between the refugee and migratory movements has been blurred, resulting in many migrants trying to enter foreign countries as refugees.

As you read, consider the following questions:

1. Why has the number of asylum seekers declined in recent years, according to Riera?

2. What were the results of the high-level dialogue on International Migration and Development held by the United Nations General Assembly in 2006, according to Riera's observance?

José Riera, "Migrants and Refugees: Why Draw a Distinction?" *United Nations Chronicle*, 2006. Copyright © 2006 United Nations. Reprinted with the permission of the United Nations.

3. What does the author assert are the important challenges faced by countries dealing with large groups of refugees and migrants?

Refugees are "migrants" in the broadest sense of the term; yet, they continue to be a distinct category of people. As specified in the 1951 Convention relating to the Status of Refugees, they are outside their country of nationality and are unable or unwilling to return due to a well-founded fear of persecution on account of race, religion, nationality or membership of a particular social group or political opinion. Over the years, the refugee concept has been broadened to encompass other people who have fled events that pose a serious threat to their life and liberty. What makes refugees different from other categories of migrants is their need for international protection and their right to seek and enjoy asylum in another state.

Refugee and migratory movements intersect in a number of different ways. People who are on the move from one country to another, even when they meet the criteria for refugee status, increasingly engage in unauthorized or undocumented movement, making use of similar routes, employing the services of the same smugglers and obtaining fraudulent travel documents from the same suppliers. While these similarities have no bearing on the fundamental difference between refugees and non-refugees, they have contributed toward a blurred distinction between the two.

Concerns about national security in the wake of 9/11 (2001) [terrorist attacks] and state efforts to stem abuse of asylum systems, as well as the growing interstate cooperation to curb irregular migration, have made it harder for refugees to seek and enjoy protection. Many states have introduced measures intended to prevent and deter foreign nationals from arriving on their territory and submitting claims for refugee status. Interdiction of boats on the high seas is a growing practice. It is also of grave concern that the restrictive measures introduced to curb irregular migration and combat human smuggling and trafficking are applied indiscriminately and prevent refugees from gaining access to asylum procedures of another state and entry to the territory.

Asylum Seekers Decrease in Numbers

The numbers speak for themselves. According to the latest asylum statistics for 36 industrialized nations published in September 2006 by the Office of the United Nations High Commissioner for Refugees (UNHCR), the downward trend in most of these countries continues unabated; 2005 saw the lowest number of asylum-seekers since 1987. During the first months of 2006, applications dropped a further 14 percent, compared to the same period last year [2005]. While this continued decline can be partially attributed to improved conditions in some of the countries of origin, it may also be due to the introduction of more restrictive asylum policies, notably in Europe.

The High-Level Dialogue on International Migration and Development, held by the UN [United Nations] General Assembly in September 2006, has undoubtedly put international migration higher on the global agenda. Participants broadly agreed that it can be a positive force for development in both countries of origin and destination, provided that it is supported by the right set of policies. They also recognized that it is essential to address the root causes of international migration to ensure that people migrated out of choice rather than necessity; the same can be said for the root causes of refugee movements. Many participants pledged to work more closely to stem irregular migration.

The presence of refugees among a larger group of migrants, some of whom may also use the asylum channel as a means of entering a foreign country, confronts the international community and UNHCR with some important challenges. High on the list of goals is an effective and coherent

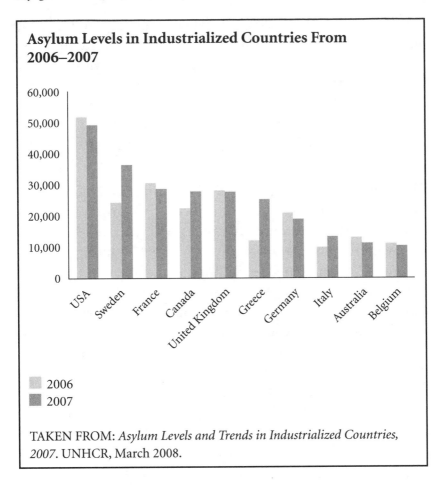

Asylum Levels in Industrialized Countries From 2006–2007

2006
2007

TAKEN FROM: *Asylum Levels and Trends in Industrialized Countries, 2007.* UNHCR, March 2008.

response to "mixed" migratory movements, including the protection of refugees and asylum-seekers. Boat movements of sub-Saharan Africans across the Mediterranean provide a good example. While the pattern of migration that we see in the Mediterranean today is not in essence a "refugee" situation, the movement of people seeking asylum and protection is one of its features. In addition to the immediate task of saving lives, systems and procedures have to be established to identify those who are in need of asylum. It is also important to ensure that any measures taken to curb irregular maritime migration do not prevent refugees from gaining the protection

to which they are entitled. Equally needed is a clearer understanding of the roles and responsibilities of the different actors involved—such as the countries of origin and transit, international organizations and shipping companies—when
people are intercepted or rescued at sea. It is also important to
ensure that people who have travelled or who hope to travel
find a lasting solution to their situation, whether or not they
are recognized as refugees.

International Law Protects Refugees' Rights

It is, of course, the legitimate right of states to control and secure their borders, but this right is not unfettered. Interception at sea and other measures to curb irregular migration
should not result in violations of the non-refoulement principle, which is the cornerstone of the international refugee regime and prevents people from being returned to countries
where their life and liberty would be at risk. It is therefore
noteworthy that the European Union's Justice and Home Affairs Ministers agreed in October 2006 that measures to reinforce the Union's southern external maritime borders and to
counter migration on the high seas must be "without preju-
dice to the principles laid down in the international legal
framework on the law of the sea and the protection of refugees".

It is important to bear in mind that refugees over time
may also become "migrants". Many have been able to establish
livelihoods and become productive members of their communities in countries of asylum. They may choose to remain in
that country, even if the causes of their flight have been removed in their homeland, or they may move on and enter the
labour market in another country. In such contexts, it is important to ensure that all refugees are able to benefit from the
human rights and labour standards to which they are entitled
as migrants. In addition, blurring the distinction between a
refugee and a migrant may even be advisable, as long as refu-

gees, who are unable to return to their country of origin, continue to receive the protection to which they are entitled under international law.

> *"Greenhouse gas emissions are changing the earth's climate, which causes natural disasters to grow more severe and more frequent, often creating a new wave of refugees fleeing climate change."*

Climate Refugees Are a Growing Problem

Teresita Perez

Teresita Perez is the deputy speechwriter for the Executive Office at American Progress. In the following essay, Perez asserts that the United States has a responsibility to provide greater financial and technical assistance to the growing number of people who have been displaced by climate change.

As you read, consider the following questions:

1. What does the author estimate is the number of climate refugees?

2. What islands had to be evacuated in 2005 because of the effects of climate change?

Teresita Perez, "Climate Refugees: The Human Toll of Global Warming," *Center for American Progress*, December 7, 2006. © 2006 Center for American Progress. This material was created by the Center for American Progress. www.americanprogress.org.

3. According to the author, what is the estimated number of people who will be displaced by climate change by 2010?

The 40,000 people displaced by this week's typhoon [in December 2006] in the Philippines are only the latest example of necessary relocation due to natural disasters. Greenhouse gas emissions are changing the earth's climate, which causes natural disasters to grow more severe and more frequent, often creating a new wave of refugees fleeing climate change.

The number of people affected is uncertain since these "climate refugees" are not granted official refugee status under the Geneva Convention, and the United Nations therefore keeps no central tally. According to the International Federation of Red Cross [and Red Crescent Societies (IFRC)], however, climate change disasters are currently a bigger cause of population displacement than war and persecution. Estimates of climate refugees currently [in 2006] range from 25 to 50 million, compared to the official refugee population of 20.8 million.

Rising sea levels, increasing desertification, weather-induced flooding, and other environmental changes, will likely displace many more hundreds of millions of people.

Accidents of geography have caused the countries least able to prevent climate change to become the most vulnerable to its earliest effects. Developing countries bear minimal responsibility for climate change because they have little industry and produce relatively small amounts [of] pollution. But their populations—often the poorest of the world's poor—are more likely to occupy dangerous locations, such as coast lines, flood plains, steep slopes, and settlements of flimsy shanty homes. The governments of these poor countries therefore carry the largest burden associated with climate refugees though they are already failing to meet the basic needs of their citizens and are ill-equipped to recover from disasters.

We can already see the effects that global warming has on some island nations. The inhabitants of the Carteret Islands were the first climate refugees forced to relocate due to sea level rise attributed to global warming. The Papua New Guinean government authorized a total evacuation of the islands in 2005—the evacuation is expected to be complete by 2007. Estimates show that by 2015 Carteret will be largely submerged and entirely uninhabitable.

Floods and other weather-related disasters have also caused nearly 10 million people to migrate from Bangladesh to India over the past two decades, creating immense population pressures. A one-meter rise in sea level—a widely predicted consequence of global warming due to an increase in the average temperatures by 2.5 to 10.4 degrees Fahrenheit over the next 40–50 years—will, in turn, inundate three million hectares in Bangladesh, and displace another 15–20 million people.

The climate refugee problem will intensify as global warming increases, potentially yielding between 150 million and 200 million refugees as early as 2010. Despite the scale of the problem, no one is really addressing the needs of these refugees, and much of the discussion about them has been limited to defining their official legal status—whether they should be officially classified as refugees or not.

We Must Take Action Now

We must act now to create an action plan that addresses the potentially devastating human toll of global warming. Climate refugees already exist and it is the moral imperative of the international community to try to ameliorate their situation. A formal extension of refugee status will be an important first step for providing a baseline of international assistance.

Inaction in the face of mounting evidence could cost billions of dollars and many innocent lives. Economist Sir Nicholas Stern released a report last month [November 2006] showing that global warming could shrink the global economy by

Protect Climate Refugees

Environmental refugees are already with us. Problems such as climate change mean they will grow in number. The choice is now between proper international management—providing protection to people forced to flee through no fault of their own—or growing international chaos. This is a plea to avoid the latter.

Molly Conisbee and Andrew Simms, Environmental Refugees: The Case for Recognition, *New Economics Foundation, 2001.*

20 percent. But taking action now to curb climate change would cost just 1 percent of global gross domestic product and ultimately give countries a huge return on their investments through the creation of new technologies, industries, and jobs.

The United States, as the largest contributor to global warming (accounting for 25 percent of the world's carbon pollution), has moral responsibility to lead the global effort to curb this phenomenon. The United States can use its economic and technical strength to transform this daunting challenge into an opportunity for innovation.

The United States must implement a bold program that both advances emerging technologies and makes greater use of existing alternative energy resources. With support from the federal government, biofuels can have a tremendous positive impact on curbing our need for oil and ameliorating the global pollution that threatens the world's most vulnerable people.

The federal government should also provide greater financial and technical assistance to help vulnerable countries prepare for climate change. Global funding to help poor countries adapt to climate change was only $0.02 billion in 2005, compared to $8 billion in subsidies to oil companies.

The United States Must Act

The United States must also implement a Plan for Global Warming Preparedness, which would include mapping out vulnerabilities via a National Global Warming Community Impact Assessment, and create state-level global warming preparedness plans.

The United States can make a great positive impact on the global climate by investing in new technologies, providing financial assistance to help prepare poorer nations, and mapping out a national preparedness plan. These three different approaches will help curtail global warming and diminish the growing population of climate refugees. Inaction is an option we can no longer afford.

> *"Climate and development are embedded evolutionary processes, and both have dynamics that should not be artificially reduced to simple cause and effect, least of all if so doing opens the way for powerful vested interests to control personal and community development."*

The Climate Refugee Problem Is Exaggerated

Mike Hulme

Mike Hulme is a professor of environmental sciences at the University of East Anglia and director of the Tyndall Centre for Climate Change Research. In the following essay, Hulme questions proposed protocols to handle climate refugees and details the way refugees are classified under the current system.

As you read, consider the following questions:

1. What are Hulme's three problems with the Recognition, Protection, and Resettlement of Climate Refugees protocol as outlined in the article?

Mike Hulme, "Climate Refugees: Cause for a New Agreement?" *Environment Magazine*, November-December 2008. Copyright © 2008 by Helen Dwight Reid Educational Foundation. Reproduced with permission of the Helen Dwight Reid Educational Foundation, published by Heldref Publications, 1319 18th Street NW, Washington, DC 20036-1802.

2. What are the problems with assigning the climate refugee category to individuals, according to the author?

3. If establishing international protocols is not the answer for Hulme, what does he propose will work when dealing with climate refugees?

With their proposed Protocol for the Recognition, Protection, and Resettlement of Climate Refugees, Frank Biermann and Ingrid Boas [a professor and a researcher in the Netherlands, respectively] make a bold and provocative suggestion, one of a number of political responses that are being floated as the world moves toward designing a new post-2012 architecture for managing climate change. Putatively a new protocol under the supervision of the UN [United Nations] Framework Convention on Climate Change, its goal would be to enable nation-states to manage proactively the resettlement of people who may face displacement due to climate change.

I see three significant flaws with the proposed protocol: the category of "climate refugee" is essentially underdetermined; it adopts a rather static view of climate-society relationships; and it is open to charges of carrying a neocolonial ideology, which guarantees it will meet political resistance.

A Series of Flaws

For the protocol to be operational, it is necessary to clearly define who does and does not fall under the designation of "climate refugee." The term implies a monocausality about the reasons for migration that just does not exist in reality. The decision to migrate is always a result of multiple interactions related to economic, political, environmental, and social factors. Even in the case of Pacific Island states such as Tuvalu, sea-level rise is rarely the decisive factor behind observed population movements, and Santa Clara University professors Michael Kevane and Leslie Gray have recently shown that the widely claimed climate-induced refugees in Darfur are nothing of the sort. One is also reminded of Nobel Laureate Amartya Sen's claim that there has never been serious famine—nor associated migrations—in a country with a democratic government and a free press.

Biermann and Boas sidestep the problem of assigning the climate refugee category to individuals by proposing that entire communities or population groups are so designated by the protocol's executive committee. They suggest such designations should ideally be a preemptive move years or even decades before the prospective critical change in climate or sea level occurs. This is certainly one way of inflating the numbers of those to be considered climate refugees—numbers which have been critiqued by many. This international committee thus could determine the fate of millions. Not only must these committee members discern, amid the enduringly fuzzy science, which habitats climate change will make unviable and by what approximate year this will occur, they also will have the even more problematic task of determining which areas "are deemed as being too difficult to protect [through adaptation] in the long-term." Adaptation is not a technical process to be determined or imposed by some distant UN committee; it is a social dynamic of change in which multiple values and power relations are at work.

A second concern regards the relationship between climate and society implied by the proposed operation of the protocol. For example, Biermann and Boas explicitly state that once categorized as climate refugees, population groups must be treated as "permanent immigrants to the regions or countries that accept them . . . [they] cannot return to their homes." This implies a frozen view of reality—once an area becomes uninhabitable it always will remain uninhabitable. Yet we know from accounts of earlier migrations in climatically stressed regions such as the Sahel in the 1970s and 1980s that migration is often a temporary response to environmental stresses. We also know that habitability is deeply contingent—

The Tuvalu Lie

[The] 10,991 poor inhabitants of Tuvalu, an island in the middle of the Pacific Ocean, have pestered the New Zealand government into accepting each and every one of them as environmental refugees, cast adrift by sea level rise from dreaded global warming. The New Zealand government took the bait. The first evacuees are scheduled to arrive next year [2002].

However, sea level around Tuvalu has been falling precipitously for the last half-century. You could look it up in the Oct. 27 [2001] issue of *Science*.

Patrick J. Michaels, "Don't Boo-Hoo for Tuvalu,"
Cato Institute, November 10, 2001. www.cato.org.

think cities such as Phoenix or Amsterdam. The imposition of irreversibility and permanency as a condition of categorization places too great a burden on being able to distinguish between human-related climate change (and sea-level rise), which is difficult to reverse, and natural, annual, or decadal climate variability, which by definition is reversible. This challenge to scientific knowledge is especially acute for all rainfall-related stresses since for most tropical regions, we continue to have little idea about the stability of local rainfall signals of anthropogenic warming. Migrations linked to storms, drought, and famine are particularly subject to this ambiguity—an ambiguity far more intractable than Biermann and Boas allow for in their optimistic claim about the "broad predictability of climate change impacts."

My third concern runs deeper still and engages with the new geopolitics of climate change. Establishing a protocol that would be supervised by an international executive committee would open up a new front in the emerging debate about green neocolonialism. New moves to establish international payments to tropical nations for preserving swathes of rainforest are also subject to this same critique of global environmental protection being used as an extension of the hegemony of international financial and political interests. In whose interests therefore is the new refugee discourse (and protocol) being developed? A recent report from the Norwegian Refugee Council alerts us to the dangers: "A fundamental critique is found in the context of North-South discourse where 'environmental security' is seen as a colonisation of the environmental problems, suggesting that the underdeveloped South poses a physical threat to the prosperous North . . . th[is] security discourse can serve to make new areas relevant for military considerations and promote repressive tendencies."

We Need a Realistic, Working Approach

Furthermore, Biermann and Boas's protocol adopts a paternalistic and centralizing approach to climate-related migration and resettlement. It is a long way removed from the participatory citizen-based dialogues between community, government, and stakeholders currently under way in countries such as the United Kingdom, where compensation for property and livelihood loss due to the encroaching sea is a live issue. A refugee regime as suggested here may only be viable in authoritative and centralized societies where the voices of citizens are rarely heard.

I remain unconvinced about the need or viability of such a protocol. Climate and development are embedded evolutionary processes, and both have dynamics that should not be artificially reduced to simple cause and effect, least of all if so doing opens the way for powerful vested interests to control personal and community development. The consequences of climate change and variability for human well-being, development, and migration are best handled within existing and evolving development and adaptation discourses and practices.

> *"Like debris from a maritime disaster, the remains of Iraq's shattered lives are washing up at border crossings, accumulating at immigration centers and settling into tenement housing."*

The Iraqi Refugee Problem Is a Crisis

Stephen Glain

Stephen Glain, a correspondent for Newsweek International, *is the author of* Mullahs, Merchants, and Militants: The Economic Collapse of the Arab World. *In the following essay, Glain maintains that one of the terrible consequences of the Iraqi war and the subsequent sectarian conflict has been a growing refugee crisis, which has implications for the entire region.*

As you read, consider the following questions:

1. According to Glain, what was the estimated number of Iraqi refugees as of 2007?

2. In what countries are Iraqi refugees concentrated, according to the author?

3. Why, does Glain explain, are Iraqi refugees such a problem in the country of Jordan?

In Damascus one recent evening [in May 2007], Ahlam Al Jaburi entered the foyer of her apartment in tears. She had risen at 5:30 A.M. that day to be first in line at the office of the United Nations High Commissioner for Refugees (UNHCR) in what she hoped would be her second interview since she first requested asylum in December [2006]. Even by the grisly standards of post-invasion Iraq, Jaburi has a strong case. In July 2005, while working with US military officers investigating the claims of war victims in the Baghdad suburb of Khadimiya, the 41-year-old computer specialist was kidnapped by three men while hailing a cab to get to work. "They called me a spy for the Americans and wanted information on their base," Jaburi says between long silences, interrupted only by the mechanical hum of a glowing fluorescent tube. "They threatened to kill me, but I had nothing to tell them." Her only concession to her tormentors was a plea that they not toss her body into the Tigris River.

Jaburi, a Sunni Muslim, was kept blindfolded and regularly beaten for eight days before her elder brother negotiated her release through a third party. The family paid a ransom of $50,000, which it drew from the *sanduk ashira*, a "tribal box" managed by local sheiks. As she was released, Jaburi, whose given name means "dream" in Arabic, was ordered to leave Iraq with her family.

Despite her service with US authorities in Baghdad, Jaburi was turned away from the US Embassy in Damascus when she requested asylum in America. After ten hours of waiting for her interview, enduring sporadic fits of pushing and shoving from other asylum seekers, she was forced to return home after the office closed for the day.

The Crisis Is a Threat to Iraq and the Surrounding Countries

The latest malignant outgrowth of [former President George W.] Bush's war in Iraq is, according to Refugees International president Ken Bacon, "the fastest-growing refugee crisis in the world." Like debris from a maritime disaster, the remains of Iraq's shattered lives are washing up at border crossings, accumulating at immigration centers and settling into tenement housing. The exodus, particularly in its first stages, has included members of Iraq's once-legendary class of skilled white-collar elites—doctors, engineers, scientists and educators. Without Iraq's professionals, it will take a generation to rebuild the country into a self-reliant state with a functioning economy.

"All of the doctors I know have decided to not go back," says a Sunni Iraqi pathologist and hospital administrator in Amman who, fearing for his family's security back home, would not give his name. "It will take a decade just to train new physicians. The insurgency has turned the country into an empty vessel, drained of talent."

What began as a thin stream of Iraqi merchants and investors seeking a safe place to do business has become [by 2007] a flood of some 2 million refugees—though it could be twice that amount—concentrated largely in Jordan and Syria. Many are destitute, and they place enormous strain on a region that is already highly combustible, both politically and economically. Once welcomed as fellow Arabs in distress, they are increasingly blamed for a scorching rise in inflation, crime, and prostitution. Heads of state and politicians warn that they will import Iraq-style sectarian strife—political fearmongering, many believe, that could become self-fulfilling at a time when the Bush administration appears to be lining up its Sunni allies for a confrontation with Iran.

"We have thousands and thousands of Iraqis spilling in from Iraq, and the government is worried that they may bring their conflict to Jordan," says Taher Masri, a respected former prime minister. "In Parliament a few weeks ago, members were condemning Iran for trying to convert Jordanians to Shiism. My driver just asked me if Shiites were a greater danger than Israelis."

Dispossession accounts for much of the Middle East's colonial inheritance, from the Ottoman Turks' genocidal eviction of Armenians to the Palestinian exodus that followed the creation of Israel with British complicity. If history is any guide—and it usually is in the Middle East—where refugees go, trouble follows. The Iraqi exodus could do more to reshape the geography and geopolitics of the region than anything gamed out in neoconservative think tanks, which tend to see the matter as an abstraction. For Jordan and Syria, themselves the bastard progeny of imperial coupling, the problem is very real—and deadly serious.

"Jordan is scared to death of the spillover from Iraq," says Rhanda Habibe, Amman bureau chief for Agence France-Presse and the doyenne of the Jordanian press corps. "The Arab world is dividing into two groups, with Egypt, Saudi Arabia, the US and Jordan on one side and Iran, Hamas and Hezbollah on the other. If there is civil war in Iraq or a civil war in the West Bank, it could all spin out of control and suck us into it."

Though there are an estimated 1.2 million Iraqi refugees in Syria, compared with some 750,000 in Jordan, the strain is felt deepest in the Hashemite Kingdom. Tiny and resource poor, Jordan is a culture dish for the Middle East's myriad schisms, scored as it is by rich and poor, Muslim and Christian, secular and fundamentalist. Jordan lumbers under the weight of a large ethnic Palestinian population—40 to 60 percent of the total—much of which is still living in camps. The Palestinians in Jordan have coexisted uneasily with indigenous "East Bankers" since the two sides went to war in 1970. The regime is burdened by its alliance with the deeply unpopular US government and its peace accord with Israel. It is also a mendicant state, unable to survive without generous aid from the United States and its Arab neighbors. In February [2007], for example, Jordan avoided a budget crisis only after Saudi Arabia, under stiff pressure from Washington, pledged $500 million in aid.

45

The Scope of the Iraqi Refugee Crisis, 2007	
Total number of Iraqi refugees	At least 2.2 million, with another 2 million displaced inside Iraq
Number of Iraqis fleeing each day	2,000
Number of Iraqi refugees in Jordan	750,000
Number of Iraqi refugees in Syria	Between 1,000,000 and 1,500,000
Number of Iraqi refugees accepted by the United States in 2007	190
Number of Iraqi refugees accepted by the U.S. who fled since 2003	Less than 100
Number of Iraqis currently working for the US government according to State and Defense Department records	118,000
Number of Iraqi translators killed according to L-3, the contractor that hires them for the US military	257

TAKEN FROM: "The Iraqi Refugee Crisis," *Human Rights First*, 2007.

The U.S. Has Done Little to Aid in the Crisis

Aside from strong-arming the Saudis, however, the White House has taken a back seat in the refugee crisis. Ellen Sauerbrey, the Assistant Secretary of State for Population, Refugees and Migration, has pushed Amman and Damascus to accommodate Iraqi exiles while doing little to open America's own borders to them. Testifying before Congress [in early 2007], Sauerbrey—who has no experience with refugees and who was appointed by Bush during a Congressional recess ... to avoid a floor fight over her strong opposition to abortion rights—confined US resettlement efforts to a single paragraph of her opening remarks. It took a measure led by Senator Edward Kennedy to shame the government into granting asylum to 7,000 Iraqi war refugees (among them, Ahlam Al Jaburi, whose persistence finally paid off this past April [2007] when she was awarded a promise of asylum).

With the US playing only a passive role in the crisis, Arab leaders are dealing with the problem as they see fit. Both Amman and Baghdad—the former worried about its capacity to absorb so many Iraqis, the latter covetous of its professional elites—are determined to reverse the migration. For a while, according to recent arrivals, Shiite men were being turned away at the Iraqi-Jordanian border, some with stamps in their passports that prohibited them from returning for five years. Now, they say, any adult male between the age of 18 and 36 stands a good chance of being refused entry. Amman recently announced it would admit only Iraqis bearing a special passport, soon to be issued by the Baghdad government on highly restricted terms.

"*Whatever the reason, the half-truths and outright misinformation that now function as conventional wisdom [about Iraq] have gravely disserved the American people.*"

The Iraqi Refugee Problem Has Been Exaggerated

Amir Taheri

Amir Taheri is the former executive editor of Kayhan, *Iran's largest daily newspaper, and a frequent contributor to numerous publications in the Middle East, Europe, and the United States. In the following essay, Taheri maintains that Americans have been victims of distortions and outright misinformation on the state of Iraq, and she outlines five measures of Iraqi political, social, and economic health.*

As you read, consider the following questions:

1. According to the author, at what countries' borders have Iraqi refugees historically queued up to enter when they flee Iraq?

2. What estimate does Taheri give for the Iraqi refugees that returned to Iraq by the end of 2005?

3. As the author reports, when did the Ashrafiayh refugee camp in Iran shut down?

Spending time in the United States after a tour of Iraq can be a disorienting experience these days. Within hours of arriving here, as I can attest from a recent visit, one is confronted with an image of Iraq that is unrecognizable. It is created in several overlapping ways: through television footage showing the charred remains of vehicles used in suicide attacks, surrounded by wailing women in black and grim-looking men carrying coffins; by armchair strategists and political gurus predicting further doom or pontificating about how the war should have been fought in the first place; by authors of instant-history books making their rounds to dissect the various "fundamental mistakes" committed by the [President George W.] Bush administration; and by reporters, co-cooned in hotels in Baghdad, explaining the "carnage" and "chaos" in the streets as signs of the country's "impending" or "undeclared" civil war. Add to all this the day's alleged scandal or revelation—an outed CIA operative, a reportedly doctored intelligence report, a leaked pessimistic assessment—and it is no wonder the American public registers disillusion with Iraq and everyone who embroiled the U.S. in its troubles.

Americans Hold Distorted Ideas

It would be hard indeed for the average interested citizen to find out on his own just how grossly this image distorts the realities of present-day Iraq. Part of the problem, faced by even the most well-meaning news organizations, is the difficulty of covering so large and complex a subject; naturally, in such circumstances, sensational items rise to the top. But even ostensibly more objective efforts, like the Brookings Institution's much-cited *Iraq Index* with its constantly updated

49

array of security, economic, and public-opinion indicators, tell us little about the actual feel of the country on the ground.

To make matters worse, many of the newsmen, pundits, and commentators on whom American viewers and readers rely to describe the situation have been contaminated by the increasing bitterness of American politics. Clearly, there are those in the media and the think tanks who wish the Iraq enterprise to end in tragedy, as a just comeuppance for George W. Bush. Others, prompted by noble sentiment, so abhor the idea of war that they would banish it from human discourse before admitting that, in some circumstances, military power can be used in support of a good cause. But whatever the reason, the half-truths and outright misinformation that now function as conventional wisdom have gravely disserved the American people.

For someone like myself who has spent considerable time in Iraq—a country I first visited in 1968—current reality there is, nevertheless, very different from this conventional wisdom, and so are the prospects for Iraq's future. It helps to know where to look, what sources to trust, and how to evaluate the present moment against the background of Iraqi and Middle Eastern history.

Five Measures on Iraq

Since my first encounter with Iraq almost 40 years ago, I have relied on several broad measures of social and economic health to assess the country's condition. Through good times and bad, these signs have proved remarkably accurate—as accurate, that is, as is possible in human affairs. For some time now, all have been pointing in an unequivocally positive direction.

The first sign is refugees. When things have been truly desperate in Iraq—in 1959, 1969, 1971, 1973, 1980, 1988, and 1990—long queues of Iraqis have formed at the Turkish and Iranian frontiers, hoping to escape. In 1973, for example, when Saddam Hussein decided to expel all those whose ancestors had not been Ottoman citizens before Iraq's creation as a state, some 1.2 million Iraqis left their homes in the space of just six weeks. This was not the temporary exile of a small group of middle-class professionals and intellectuals, which is a common enough phenomenon in most Arab countries. Rather, it was a departure *en masse* [all together], affecting people both in small villages and in big cities, and it was a scene regularly repeated under Saddam Hussein.

Since the toppling of Saddam in 2003, this is one highly damaging image we have not seen on our television sets—and we can be sure that we *would* be seeing it if it were there to be shown. To the contrary, Iraqis, far from fleeing, have been returning home. By the end of 2005, in the most conservative estimate, the number of returnees topped the 1.2-million mark. Many of the camps set up for fleeing Iraqis in Turkey, Iran, and Saudi Arabia since 1959 have now closed down. The oldest such center, at Ashrafiayh in southwest Iran, was formally shut when its last Iraqi guests returned home in 2004.

A second dependable sign likewise concerns human movement, but of a different kind. This is the flow of religious pilgrims to the Shiite shrines in Karbala and Najaf. Whenever things start to go badly in Iraq, this stream is reduced to a trickle and then it dries up completely. From 1991 (when Saddam Hussein massacred Shiites involved in a revolt against him) to 2003, there were scarcely any pilgrims to these cities. Since Saddam's fall, they have been flooded with visitors. In 2005, the holy sites received an estimated 12 million pilgrims, making them the most visited spots in the entire Muslim world, ahead of both Mecca and Medina.

Over 3,000 Iraqi clerics have also returned from exile, and Shiite seminaries, which just a few years ago held no more than a few dozen pupils, now boast over 15,000 from 40 different countries. This is because Najaf, the oldest center of Shiite scholarship, is once again able to offer an alternative to

Iraqi Refugees Are Returning

The most dramatic sign of improvement in Iraq can be seen in the number of Iraqi refugees who fled the violence at the height of the war and are now returning home in increasing numbers. Most of these returning Iraqis do so with the knowledge that their land is still a dangerous place, that the war is not over and that al Qaeda killers still have the power to strike.

But there is a sense that the tide has turned.

Donald Lambro, "Dems in Denial Over Iraq Recovery," Townhall.com, November 26, 2007. http://townhall.com.

Qom, the Iranian "holy city" where a radical and highly politicized version of Shiism is taught. Those wishing to pursue the study of more traditional and quietist forms of Shiism now go to Iraq where, unlike in Iran, the seminaries are not controlled by the government and its secret police.

Economic and Agricultural Indicators

A third sign, this one of the hard economic variety, is the value of the Iraqi dinar [currency], especially as compared with the region's other major currencies. In the final years of Saddam Hussein's rule, the Iraqi dinar was in free fall; after 1995, it was no longer even traded in Iran and Kuwait. By contrast, the new dinar, introduced early in 2004, is doing well against both the Kuwaiti dinar and the Iranian rial [currency], having risen by 17 percent against the former and by 23 percent against the latter. Although it is still impossible to fix its value against a basket of international currencies, the new Iraqi dinar has done well against the U.S. dollar, increasing in value by almost 18 percent between August 2004 and August

2005. The overwhelming majority of Iraqis, and millions of Iranians and Kuwaitis, now treat it as a safe and solid medium of exchange.

My fourth time-tested sign is the level of activity by small- and medium-sized businesses. In the past, whenever things have gone downhill in Iraq, large numbers of such enterprises have simply closed down, with the country's most capable entrepreneurs decamping to Jordan, Syria, Saudi Arabia, the Persian Gulf states, Turkey, Iran, and even Europe and North America. Since liberation, however, Iraq has witnessed a private-sector boom, especially among small- and medium-sized businesses.

According to the International Monetary Fund (IMF) and the World Bank, as well as numerous private studies, the Iraqi economy has been doing better than any other in the region. The country's gross domestic product rose to almost $90 billion in 2004 (the latest year for which figures are available), more than double the output for 2003, and its real growth rate, as estimated by the IMF, was 52.3 percent. In that same period, exports increased by more than $3 billion, while the inflation rate fell to 25.4 percent, down from 70 percent in 2002. The unemployment rate was halved, from 60 percent to 30 percent.

Related to this is the level of agricultural activity. Between 1991 and 2003, the country's farm sector experienced unprecedented decline, in the end leaving almost the entire nation dependent on rations distributed by the United Nations under Oil-for-Food. [Since 2004], by contrast, Iraqi agriculture has undergone an equally unprecedented revival. Iraq now exports foodstuffs to neighboring countries, something that has not happened since the 1950s. Much of the upturn is due to smallholders who, shaking off the collectivist system imposed by the Baathists, have retaken control of land that was confiscated decades ago by the state.

Freedom of Speech Abounds

Finally, one of the surest indices of the health of Iraqi society has always been its readiness to talk to the outside world. Iraqis are a verbalizing people; when they fall silent, life is incontrovertibly becoming hard for them. There have been times, indeed, when one could find scarcely a single Iraqi, whether in Iraq or abroad, prepared to express an opinion on anything remotely political. This is what [Iraqi academic] Kanan Makiya meant when he described Saddam Hussein's regime as a "republic of fear."

Today, again by way of dramatic contrast, Iraqis are voluble to a fault. Talk radio, television talk shows, and Internet blogs are all the rage, while heated debate is the order of the day in shops, teahouses, bazaars, mosques, offices, and private homes. A "catharsis" is how Luay Abdulilah, the Iraqi short-story writer and diarist, describes it. "This is one way of taking revenge against decades of deadly silence." Moreover, a vast network of independent media has emerged in Iraq, including over 100 privately owned newspapers and magazines and more than two dozen radio and television stations. To anyone familiar with the state of the media in the Arab world, it is a truism that Iraq today is the place where freedom of expression is most effectively exercised.

"Has the 'War on Terror' been trumped by the [President George W.] Bush Administration's mad drive to make America safe for immigration?"

Refugees Are a Significant National Security Threat

Thomas Allen

Thomas Allen is a contributor to VDARE.com, a Webzine that advocates reduced immigration. In the following essay, Allen argues that the immigration policy of the United States is too lax toward refugees from areas that provide material support for terrorism. The result, he asserts, might compromise the larger "War on Terror" and could endanger American national security.

As you read, consider the following questions:

1. As Allen reports, how many Burmese Karens were resettled in the United States in 2006?

2. According to the author, how did this resettlement interfere with the USA PATRIOT Act?

Thomas Allen, "Bush Administration: What War on Terror? Bring on the Immigrants!" VDARE.com, August 28, 2006. Copyright © 2006 VDARE.com. Reproduced by permission. www.vdare.com.

3. How did Secretary of State Condoleezza Rice resolve the problem between the resettlement and the Patriot Act, according to Allen?

Somalis are using United Nations [UN] refugee camps in Zambia as 'stepping stones' to "other destinations," i.e. the U.S., according to the Secretary of the Zambian ministry of the Interior, Peter Mumba.

Speaking to the UN news service, the Integrated Regional Information Network (IRIN), Mr. Mumba explained that the Somalis first settle in Meheba, Zambia's largest refugee camp and then, either bribing their way out or with assistance from Somalis outside the camp, slip into neighboring Zimbabwe and Namibia. From there they filter into South Africa, boarding ships bound . . . for Mexico. According to the Secretary, "once in Mexico, they can easily walk into the USA as their final destination."

The Zambian government has written the South African, Namibian and Zimbabwean governments to be on the look out for Somali refugees. But apparently, the Zambians know it would be futile to warn the U.S. government about the illegal traffic from Somalia—although the country is a known base for al Qaeda [an Islamist extremist movement] and related Wahhabi militant groups.

Immigration Is Dangerous

Has the "War on Terror" been trumped by the [President George W.] Bush Administration's mad drive to make America safe for immigration?

That wouldn't be surprising. The War on Terror takes a back seat to immigration enthusiasm in many ways.

Another example: This summer [2006] the U.S. began the resettlement of about 9,300 Burmese Karens from a refugee camp in Thailand to the U.S.

As usual, once a decision has been made to resettle a group to the U.S., all obstacles along the path were cleared away. The

The Doors Are Open Too Wide for Immigrants

While the open borders lobby—which now perhaps should more appropriately be known simply as the "Treason Lobby"—has for years ignored, sneered at and denounced as "racists" and "xenophobes" anyone who warned of the consequences of mass immigration, some of those consequences became agonizingly clear on Sept. 11 [2001, when terrorist hijackers crashed passenger airplanes into the World Trade Center and the Pentagon].

Sam Francis,
"Immigration Reform Prophets vs. the Treason Lobby,"
VDARE.com, September 27, 2001. www.vdare.com.

usual questions about capacity to absorb an influx are thrown out the window by the refugees' instant access to all welfare. The extensive network of federal "refugee contractors"—which the public thinks of as private charities but which have actually been captured by the federal government—are paid to hand out money from dozens of government programs.

The U.S. public health service has committed to curing cases of TB [tuberculosis] in camps before infected individuals are resettled—a commitment it has made and failed to fulfill in the past. The immigration bar for individuals with HIV has been waived for refugees under a [President Bill] Clinton Executive Order—which the Bush Administration typically has let stand.

But now it turns out that even the recently re-authorized Patriot Act can be ignored when it interferes with the refugee resettlement process.

The Patriot Act broadly defines terms such as "terrorist activity" and "terrorist organization." It includes "material support" for a "terrorist organization" as grounds for prosecution under the act. And, according to Assistant Attorney General Rachel Brand, the Justice Department uses the material support clause to deport aliens or bar entry when other means cannot be found.

The loosely defined terms provided by the Patriot Act have proven to be useful tools for the Justice Department in its prosecution and removal of foreign Jihadists in the U.S.

Karen Tribesman Are a Risk

But many of the Karen tribesmen have provided material support to an organization—the Karen National Army—which is on the State Department's list of terrorist organizations.

The Department of Homeland Security initially found "thousands" in the group were inadmissible to the U.S. under the Patriot Act.

Got immigrant terrorists? No problem! Just before resettlement was to begin in June [2006], Secretary of State [Condoleezza] Rice simply waived the Patriot Act terrorist provisions for the entire group. She ordered them to be admitted pretty much "as is"—ignoring the concerns of officials in the Justice Department.

No doubt Patriot Act definitions of a terrorist organization and material support are overly broad. And it may be true that, as supporters of the waiver claim, material support was provided unwittingly or under coercion—in some cases, but far from all.

This Decision Undermines the Patriot Act

If the Patriot Act is a bad law, then it is a bad law in all cases, not just in some cases.

Rice's blanket waiver makes no distinction among members in the group. Like the group designation of refugee status, it significantly widens the avenue for refugee admission, which was originally meant for those who qualify on the basis of a case-by-case evaluation, not owing to membership in a group.

At the very least, the waiver will complicate, if not end, the use of a legal tool designed for the pursuit of "terrorists."

At worst, it suggests the government is moving to apply a law to U.S. citizens while ignoring it for some immigrants.

It now seems that many if not most future refugee groups will get an automatic blanket waiver of Patriot Act provisions—especially those from the Middle East and Muslim regions of Africa.

Yes, Virginia (Dare) [the first English child to be born in America in 1587 and the individual for whom this Webzine is named], the War on Terror has indeed been put on hold to meet the demands of the Bush Administration and refugee contractors for a larger influx of refugees.

> *"There is still time to pass legislation, or reform the Immigration and Nationality Act, to apply definitions that don't turn victims of terrorism into supposed terrorists themselves."*

Refugees Are Not a Serious National Security Threat

Anna Husarska

Anna Husarska is the senior policy advisor at the International Rescue Committee. In the following essay, she perceives U.S. immigration law, as it pertains to refugees, as further victimizing those who suffer from violence and aggression. She cites three specific cases of Iraqi refugees hoping to resettle in the United States, and she speculates on how U.S. Department of Homeland Security would interrogate these individuals to ascertain whether they are victims or supporters of terrorism.

As you read, consider the following questions:

1. Why is the U.S. government keeping out many Iraqi refugees, according to the author?

2. What does the author perceive as the flaw in U.S. immigration law that allows this injustice to happen?

Anna Husarska, "Victims of Terror Aren't Terrorists," *Los Angeles Times*, April 23, 2007. Copyright © 2007 Los Angeles Times. Reproduced by permission.

3. How does the material support determinant figure into the first case of Iraqi refugees cited in the article?

The civil war in Iraq has stranded 2 million Iraqi refugees in neighboring countries—and Washington says that up to 7,000 of them may be resettled in the United States this year [2007].

But which ones?

During a recent trip to the Middle East, I talked with many refugees who seemed to deserve resettlement in the U.S. but may never get it. Even though they have been brutalized by the factional fighting in Iraq, the U.S. government might label them supporters of terrorism.

Here is how it happens. After the United Nations or another nongovernmental agency determines that a person has a "well-founded fear of persecution" in his country of origin, the refugee is interviewed by officials from the U.S. Department of Homeland Security. The screening process includes detailed questions to make sure all of the anti-terrorism provisions of the Patriot Act and the REAL ID Act are met.

This is understandable—but there is a flaw in the laws. The definition of who provides "material support" to terrorists is unreasonably broad. There have been several legislative attempts to fix it, but the provisions still stand, largely unchanged, preventing resettlement of Iraqis like these three I met in February and March [2007].

Wrongly Interpreted Circumstances

The liquor store owner is a Christian Iraqi. In July [2006], he found a threatening note slipped under the door of his store in Baghdad. (Selling alcohol violates Islamic law.) The police could not help. With no other means of supporting his wife and seven children still at home, he kept the shop open. The next week, five men entered the store, beat him, emptied the cash register, took his cell phone and demanded $10,000. Four

61

The U.S. Commitment to Refugees

The Refugee resettlement program is an enormously important foreign policy tool. Its use can also promote acceptance of other durable solutions: repatriation and local integration. We are doing our best to ensure the program is flexible and that we provide access to refugees for whom resettlement is the appropriate durable solution. It is the Administration's view that important national security concerns and counter-terrorism efforts are compatible with our historic role as the world's leader in refugee resettlement.

Ellen Sauerbrey,
"Oversight of U.S. Refugee Admissions and Policy,"
Testimony Before the Senate Judiciary Committee
Subcommittee on Immigration, Border Security,
and Citizenship, September 27, 2006.

days later, kidnappers snatched his 1-year-old son and demanded a ransom of $30,000. With the help of an adult son in Australia, he raised $10,000 and delivered it as instructed. The next morning he found a package on the porch: one plastic bag with the head of his son and another with a little beheaded body. The liquor store owner buried his son, and the family fled Iraq as soon as they got their travel documents.

What the Americans will want to know is whether the kidnappers were just after cash. Those who act "for mere personal monetary gain" have not committed "terrorist activities." Then—and only then—would paying them a ransom not be considered "material support of terrorist activities."

The civil engineer is a Sunni Iraqi whose family lived in a Shiite neighborhood. After the U.S. invasion, he got a job with an American company doing reconstruction work. He was abducted by Shiite militiamen. For 21 days, his family searched desperately for him, calling anyone who might pull strings to get him back. To thank those who came to their aid, they gave out prepaid minutes for cell phones, sent by text-messaging a code that could be redeemed with the phone company. In all, they gave out $3,000 worth of credits, some of which went to the kidnappers.

That may have helped get the engineer released. The engineer also used his own cell phone while he was held captive—an important detail. He was freed unharmed and left the country.

The critical question here will be: Were the cell phone minutes to the kidnappers sent from the engineer's phone or from that of a relative? To transfer any form of payment to a terrorist is to "materially support terrorist activities." If the bribe were sent by a relative, the engineer probably won't be accused of "supporting terrorism"—unless he asked the relative to give the bribe.

The hairdresser is a single mother. She received threats by phone and in writing. She was told to close her salon, judged as unacceptable by Muslim extremists. In 2005, a man in a black hood entered her shop, beat her, pulled the crucifix off her neck, and raped her. A week later, her son was kidnapped and the same man called; she recognized his voice. He demanded $10,000. She gathered $7,000 and paid the ransom. Her son was returned, and she fled the country with him.

At issue here is whether the rapist/kidnapper is a member of a U.S. government-documented terrorist group. Even ransom can constitute "material support" of terrorists. But if money is given "under duress" to a group that is not on either of the two State Department lists of foreign terrorist groups, the "material support" restriction can be waived.

The U.S. Shares Responsibility for the Initial Victimizations

Over the last year [2006-2007], I traveled to half a dozen countries in Africa and Asia and saw bona fide refugees barred from entering the U.S. because of obstacles that seem similarly absurd. But the U.S. government bears special responsibility for the war in Iraq, so the mindless application of "material support" provisions to Iraqi victims of terrorism would be particularly deplorable.

The first of the 7,000 Iraqi refugees to be resettled this year [2007] in the U.S. has yet to arrive. So, there is still time to pass legislation, or reform the Immigration and Nationality Act, to apply definitions that don't turn victims of terrorism into supposed terrorists themselves.

Periodical Bibliography

Anna Badkhen   "Displaced Iraqis to Return—but to Where?" Salon.com, June 12, 2008.

Doug Bandow   "Religious Persecution's Global Reach," *The American Spectator*, May 22, 2007.

Kit Batten, Kari Manlove, and Nat Gryl   "Climate Refugees: Global Warming Will Spur Migration," Center for American Progress, July 3, 2007.

Alexandra Berzon   "Tuvalu Is Drowning," Salon.com, March 31, 2006.

Elizabeth Dinovella   "Iraq's Forgotten Refugees," *The Progressive*, September 2008.

David Enders   "'We Are Afraid to Return,'" *Mother Jones*, April 27, 2006.

Joseph P. Hoar   "Abandoned at the Border," *The New York Times*, August 31, 2007.

Bruce E. Johansen   "From Baffin Island to New Orleans," *The Progressive*, December 2005.

Michael Kamber   "Afghanistan's Environmental Casualties," *Mother Jones*, March 6, 2002.

Donald Lambro   "Dems in Denial over Iraqi Recovery," Townhall.com, November 26, 2007.

James R. Lee   "Global Warming Is Just the Tip of the Iceberg," *The Washington Post*, January 4, 2009.

Michael Schwartz   "Iraq's Tidal Wave of Misery," *Mother Jones*, February 11, 2008.

Brenda Walker   "World Refugee Day: Mondo Multicult—Courtesy of the UN and the Bush White House," VDARE.com, July 1, 2008.

OPPOSING
VIEWPOINTS®
SERIES

CHAPTER 2

Who Is Responsible for Aiding Refugees?

Chapter Preface

There are many reasons that people flee from their homes and become refugees. Some individuals migrate to escape persecution; others to find food and shelter; and some to escape violent conflict that threatens their very existence. Once a refugee has made the difficult decision to leave his or her home and has made an often demanding journey to a refugee camp or a neighboring country, what governing or organizational entity has the responsibility to provide help for them? Experts in the field agree this is a complicated debate based on a number of factors, and further assert that there are three main sources of help for refugees: national governments, nongovernmental organizations (NGOs), and the international community.

Many believe that national governments are responsible for the well-being of refugees within their borders. That means that if, for example, Cuban refugees came over on boats from Cuba and landed in Miami, the United States government would have the responsibility not only to clothe, feed, shelter, and protect them, but also to integrate them into local communities and guide them through the asylum or immigration process. In some cases, national governments might also return them to their homeland or resettle them in another country. Whatever the outcome, the United States would assume the responsibility and cost for any refugee that ends up inside its borders.

In some instances, however, national governments are unwilling or unable to assume the obligation of aiding refugees within their own borders. In such cases, commentators emphasize the role the international community must play in helping refugees. Coalitions of national governments, under the aegis of the United Nations, can take on a leadership role in providing humanitarian aid, protection, legal assistance, and resettlement services to large groups of refugees anywhere in the world.

One such international organization was created for just such a purpose. Established on December 14, 1950, the United Nations High Commissioner for Refugees (UNHCR) was mandated to lead and coordinate international action to alleviate the worldwide refugee crisis. The organization also provides humanitarian assistance and resettlement services for refugees and internally displaced persons (IDPs), who are considered to be refugees displaced but still residing in their own country.

Another group tasked with the obligation to help refugees are NGOs, which are non-governmental organizations independent from national governments and the international community. NGOs involved with the refugee issue are usually focused in two areas: humanitarian aid and protection issues. Most have developed a deep knowledge of specific issues in a regional area and can draw from a deep pool of resources.

The following chapter explores the advantages and disadvantages of each sector, weighing which can provide the best help to alleviate the refugee problem. The authors of the viewpoints also consider the controversial role UNHCR plays in refugee assistance and debate whether the United States should be doing more to help refugees worldwide.

"With . . . resources at their disposal, refugees will be able to live a more productive and rewarding life and prepare for their future, wherever that might be."

The International Community Should Help Alleviate the Refugee Problem

António Guterres

In the viewpoint that follows, António Guterres discusses the precarious situations more than 6 million refugees face today: extensive camp stays, the inability to repatriate, inadequate health care and education, and human trafficking and violence. In response, he gives a three-step plan for the international community to encourage peace in turbulent countries and to enable refugees to take control of their lives and their futures. From 1995 to 2002, Guterres was prime minister of Portugal, and in 2005 he was appointed United Nations High Commissioner for Refugees (UNHCR).

António Guterres, "Refugees Are the Responsibility of the Whole International Community," Telegraph.co.uk, December 10, 2008. © Copyright of Telegraph Media Group Limited 2009. Reproduced by permission.

As you read, consider the following questions:

1. According to the UNHCR, what are some of the limitations refugees face even after they have resettled in a developed country?

2. What are some of the dangers Guterres names that refugees find during further migration or resettlement in urban areas?

3. How might the United Nations help to decrease violence in countries that produce refugees, according to the High Commissioner?

Refugees are a symbol of our turbulent times. As each new conflict erupts, the world's newspapers and television screens are filled with pictures of masses on the move, fleeing from their own country with just the clothes on their back and the few possessions they are able to carry. Those who survive the journey depend on the willingness of neighbouring states to open their borders and the ability of humanitarian organizations to provide the new arrivals with food, shelter and other basic needs.

But what happens once the exodus is over, the journalists have packed their bags and the world has turned its attention to the next crisis? In the vast majority of cases, the refugees are left behind, obliged to spend the best years of their lives in shabby camps and shanty settlements, exposed to all kind of dangers and with serious restrictions placed upon their rights and freedoms.

Refugees Face Long-Term Dangers

The problem of protracted refugee situations has reached enormous proportions. According to UNHCR's [United Nations High Commissioner for Refugees'] most recent statistics, some six million people (excluding the special case of more than four million Palestinian refugees) have now been living in exile for five years or longer. More than 30 of these situations are to be found throughout the world, the vast majority of them in African and Asian countries which are struggling to meet the needs of their own citizens.

Many of these refugees are effectively trapped in the camps and communities where they are accommodated. They cannot go home because their countries of origin—Afghanistan, Iraq, Myanmar, Somalia and Sudan for example—are at war or are affected by serious human rights violations. Only a tiny proportion has the chance of being resettled in Australia, Canada, the UK [United Kingdom], the USA [United States] or another developed country. And in most cases, the authorities in their countries where they have found refuge will not allow them to integrate with the local population or to become citizens of those states.

During their long years in exile, these refugees are confronted with a very harsh and difficult life. In some cases they have no freedom of movement, do not have access to land and are forbidden from finding a job. As time passes, the international community loses interest in such situations. Funding dries up and essential services such as education and health care stagnate and then deteriorate.

Packed into overcrowded settlements, deprived of an income and with little to occupy their time, these refugee populations are afflicted by all kinds of social ills, including prostitution, rape and violence. Unsurprisingly, and despite the restrictions placed upon them, many take the risk of moving to an urban area or trying to migrate to another country, putting themselves in the dangerous hands of human smugglers and traffickers.

Refugees' children suffer enormously in such circumstances. A growing proportion of the world's exiles have been born and raised in the artificial environment of a refugee camp, their parents unable to work and in many cases reliant upon the meagre rations provided by international aid agen-

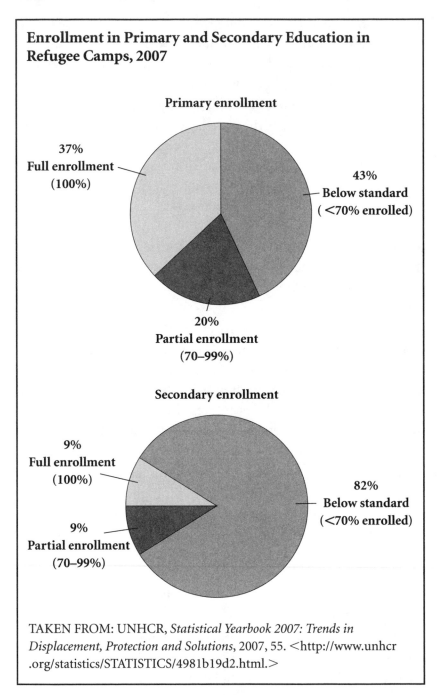

Enrollment in Primary and Secondary Education in Refugee Camps, 2007

Primary enrollment

37%
Full enrollment
(100%)

43%
Below standard
(<70% enrolled)

20%
Partial enrollment
(70–99%)

Secondary enrollment

9%
Full enrollment
(100%)

82%
Below standard
(<70% enrolled)

9%
Partial enrollment
(70–99%)

TAKEN FROM: UNHCR, *Statistical Yearbook 2007: Trends in Displacement, Protection and Solutions*, 2007, 55. <http://www.unhcr .org/statistics/STATISTICS/4981b19d2.html.>

cies. And even if peace returns to their country of origin, these children will go back to a 'homeland' which they have never seen and where they may not even speak the local language.

I consider it intolerable that the human potential of so many people is being wasted during their time in exile and imperative that steps are taken to provide them with a solution to their plight.

An International Responsibility

First, a concerted effort is required to halt the armed conflicts and human rights violations that force people to flee from their country and oblige them to live as refugees. In this respect, the UN [United Nations] has a particularly important role to play, whether by means of mediation, negotiation, the establishment of peacekeeping missions or the punishment of those who are found guilty of war crimes.

Second, while funding may be scarce as a result of the financial crisis, every effort must be made to improve conditions for the world's long-term refugees, whether they are living in camps, rural or urban areas. Particular emphasis should be placed on providing exiled populations with livelihoods, education and training. With these resources at their disposal, refugees will be able to live a more productive and rewarding life and prepare for their future, wherever that might be.

Finally, while we will not solve the world's protracted refugee situations by moving all of the people concerned to the more developed regions of the world, the richer nations should demonstrate their solidarity with countries that host large numbers of refugees by resettling a proportion of them, especially those whose security and welfare is at greatest risk. The UK's Gateway Protection Programme is one such resettlement initiative aiming to protect 750 vulnerable refugees a year by bringing them to Britain.

The refugee problem is a responsibility of the international community as a whole, and can only be effectively tackled by means of collective and cooperative action.

We must ensure that the assistance provided to refugees also brings tangible benefits to local populations. We must encourage the international community to provide adequate support to those countries that are prepared to naturalize refugees and give them citizenship. And we must establish more effective approaches to the return and reintegration of refugees in their countries of origin, thereby enabling them to benefit from and contribute to the peace-building process.

"The United States, in keeping with a national government's responsibility to protect refugees within its territory, has a strong asylum system and strives to help other nations develop similar systems."

National Governments Have an Obligation to Refugees

David Anthony Denny

David Anthony Denny is a staff writer at USINFO, a production of the Bureau of International Information Programs, U.S. Department of State. In the following essay, Denny reports that U.S. Department of State officials believe that protecting refugees is an obligation of national governments, working independently and in conjunction with the Office of the United Nations High Commissioner for Refugees (UNHCR).

As you read, consider the following questions:

1. How does the United States help other countries improve their treatment of refugees and asylum seekers,

David Anthony Denny, "Protecting Refugees a National Obligation," America.gov, May 8, 2007. Reproduced by permission. www.america.gov.

according to Kelly Ryan, a deputy assistant secretary of state in the Bureau of Population, Refugee and Migration Affairs?

2. How does Ryan say the United Nations High Commissioner for Refugees (UNHCR) can help refugees?

3. What is the relationship between UNHCR and the United States, according to Ryan?

The United States, in keeping with a national government's responsibility to protect refugees within its territory, has a strong asylum system and strives to help other nations develop similar systems, according to a State Department official.

Kelly Ryan, a deputy assistant secretary of state in the Bureau of Population, Refugee and Migration Affairs, told the American Enterprise Institute (AEI) May 4 [2007] that the United States has "a very robust asylum system with many review levels. I think it's the best in the world."

The United States Takes on an Advisory Role

The United States talks to other countries about their asylum systems and has worked with the UN [United Nations] High Commissioner for Refugees (UNHCR) doing joint training programs with Mexico and Central America, she said. The United States also has advised various countries on the development of their asylum laws and has a very good relationship with many countries that are just beginning to have a formalized asylum system, Ryan said.

"We've had one [an asylum system] in place for quite some time, and we've had experiences where we've been successful, and we've had experiences where we needed to change a certain procedure because we were getting an outcome we weren't entirely satisfied with," she said.

The U.S. Role in Aiding Refugees

With an annual budget of roughly $1 billion for refugee assistance, the United States is the world's largest single-country donor to efforts to aid refugees and internally displaced persons. Most of that money goes to the UN-HCR [United Nations High Commissioner for Refugees], which receives 22 percent of its funding from the United States, and other international organizations.

Jane Morse, "Protecting Refugees a High U.S. Priority," *America.gov, December 16, 2008. www.america.gov.*

Ryan, during her 10 years at the Department of Justice handling the application of asylum law in the United States, worked very closely with UNHCR. That organization gives the United States supervisory advice on its obligations under international conventions, particularly the 1951 Convention relating to the Status of Refugees and its 1967 protocol.

According to Ryan, UNHCR mobilizes national governments to help and protect refugees, but "there are rogue states throughout the world that are unwilling or unable to help refugees," she said.

"UNHCR is there, as is the United States, trying to make sure that refugees are protected from physical or mental harm, from forced return, and from being disadvantaged by their status," she said.

In promoting international protection of refugees, the United States believes UNHCR performs a very valuable function, Ryan said.

"There are places in the world where the United States is not welcomed, liked or influential," she said, and in those places UNHCR can be a particularly effective advocate for refugee protection. There are also places where the United States is more effective than UNHCR. In those places, the United States shares its information with UNHCR and works collegially. On other occasions the two entities can accomplish more together than if they worked separately, Ryan said.

Ryan described the overall relationship between the U.S. government and UNHCR as "very respectful," and said the agency was also "very responsive" to U.S. requests.

However, Ryan said, on occasion UNHCR has disagreed with positions taken by the U.S. government and has filed *amicus curiae* [friend of the court] briefs with the U.S. Supreme Court when U.S. government policies faced legal challenges. Such filings, submitted by parties not directly involved in the litigation, offer additional information the court might wish to consider in reaching its decision.

Ryan said the United States is UNHCR's largest bilateral donor and works with UNHCR throughout the year to talk about priorities for the United States. In addition, the United States is assisting UNHCR in voluntary refugee returns in southern Sudan, Afghanistan and Liberia, "where people are finally able to return home and begin their new lives," she said.

Darfur and Chad Receive Important Aid

The United States also is helping UNHCR continue its work in Sudan's Darfur region and in Chad, and is cooperating with the UN agency on the humanitarian corridors created in Lebanon to permit access by the International Committee of the Red Cross and those providing humanitarian aid to victims of the conflict. The United States has worked on local integration, though this is not greatly welcomed by some states. Ryan said a recent example of refugee resettlement and local integration efforts coming together occurred with Burmese refugees in Thailand.

John Bolton, former U.S. ambassador to the United Nations and now an AEI senior fellow, also said national governments are accountable for refugees. The fact that many governments leave deciding who qualifies as a refugee to UNHCR constitutes "ducking the hard political choices," he said.

> "NGOs can ... be present, witness, monitor, document, report, advise, influence, and 'responsibilise' states and government actors, thereby contributing to the protection and well-being of people affected by forced displacement."

Non-Governmental Organizations Have an Obligation to Refugees

Ed Schenkenberg van Mierop

Ed Schenkenberg van Mierop is the coordinator of the International Council of Voluntary Agencies (ICVA), a global network of humanitarian and developmental non-governmental organizations (NGOs). In the following essay, he elucidates many of the ways NGOs have protected refugees and outlines how NGOs can complement the aid to refugees given by the United Nations High Commissioner of Refugees (UNHCR).

As you read, consider the following questions:

1. According to the author, what are the "two inextricably linked pillars" of humanitarian response?

2. As the author reports, when did NGOs begin to seriously develop an interest in the protection of refugees?

3. What does the author believe are the feelings many NGOs have toward the United Nations High Commissioner of Refugees' policies?

The international protection of the majority of the world's refugees has traditionally been the domain of the UN [United Nations] High Commissioner for Refugees (UNHCR). For some time, however, several operational humanitarian non-governmental organizations (NGOs) have claimed territory in this area as well. They have developed protection policies and/or designated protection capacities within their offices and field teams. The question is, as a result, are these NGOs and UNHCR working as competitors or companions?

Humanitarian response in general is founded on two inextricably linked pillars: assistance and protection. "Humanitarian assistance" is aid to a disaster or crisis-affected population—in this case, refugees—that primarily seeks to save lives and alleviate human suffering. "Protection" of refugees, in contrast, aims to ensure full respect for the rights of this refugee population in accordance with international human rights law and refugee law.

NGOs and Refugees: A History

While historically, human rights NGOs and refugee councils have always been involved in the protection of refugees, the interest of humanitarian NGOs in protection issues developed in the mid-1990s. In this period, several large humanitarian NGOs blamed UNHCR for focusing on the provision of assistance at the expense of its protection mandate, particularly in the Balkans. In Central Africa, too, UNHCR and NGOs were faced with a crisis in protection. Among the refugees in the camps in (then) Eastern Zaire and Tanzania were many who, in fact, should have been excluded from refugee status because they were implicated in the Rwandan genocide in 1994. Humanitarian NGOs publicly questioned how UNHCR could execute its mandate in such a situation. Several of them published reports or made public statements in which they denounced violations of the rights of Rwandan refugees, and there were even a few NGOs that left the camps in Tanzania and Zaire.

Some eight years later, many of the same NGOs have a deep engagement in protection. They have realized that humanitarian action is more than providing relief, or "truck and chuck," as one large NGO internally calls it. Humanitarian staff must have an eye for the human rights context in which they operate and for the impact of their operations on the rights of the people for and with whom they work.

Last December [2004], representatives from some 12 large humanitarian NGOs and senior UNHCR officials discussed their relationship when it comes to protection. UNHCR's main question for this meeting was how NGOs understood their role in protection. The NGOs wanted to know if UNHCR was really open to collaboration on protection.

Such UNHCR-NGO discussions are not new. The same questions came up in the past. In the early 1990s, UNHCR and NGOs drew up a highly ambitious plan for a "partnership in action" (PARinAC), which included recommendations for the coordination of protection activities, the joint development of protection priorities and strategies, and the strengthening of the complementarity of UNHCR and NGO protection activities. The PARinAC process, however, dealt more with the general and operational aspects of the UNHCR-NGO relationship than with the specific aspects of protection.

In the late 1990s, UNHCR involved NGOs in the "Reach Out Process on International Protection." This process was set up by UNHCR to respond to the mid-1990s protection crisis and to find renewed commitment from states and others for the refugee agency's mandate. Meetings with NGOs in New

York, Bangkok, and Nairobi were, unfortunately, given little follow-up and the objective of "developing a common protection agenda" was never realized.

Nevertheless, some progress was made. A field guide for NGOs on refugee protection was jointly produced with UN-HCR. In addition, UNHCR and various NGOs worked together on the "Global Consultations on International Protection" to mark the 50th anniversary of the 1951 UN Convention relating to the Status of Refugees.

Collaboration Is Essential

As was recognized at the recent meeting between UNHCR and the dozen NGOs, there is every reason now to engage in further practical collaboration in a much more coherent fashion than ever before. At a time when international refugee protection is severely constrained for political and financial reasons, protection in the humanitarian sector is one of its weakest points. Basic failures still exist in field operations. The registration of refugees, a prerequisite for effective protection, is not always undertaken. Furthermore, many have noted the severe shortage of experienced UNHCR protection officers. In recent years, several NGOs have responded to these shortcomings by developing additional protection capacities, for example, the inter-agency training process on refugee law for NGO staff—the Reach Out Refugee Protection Training Project—and the International Rescue Committee's Surge Project to strengthen UNHCR's operational protection presence. However, such efforts alone cannot really provide a long-term solution to the problem.

Other protection measures, such as the separation of armed elements from refugees or the relocation of refugee camps away from international borders, cannot be carried out by NGOs or UNHCR because these measures go far beyond their mandates and capacities.

The Role of NGOs

Non-governmental organisations (NGOs) may not be specifically mandated through international conventions to offer protection to refugees. Through their work, however, many NGOs operate under mission statements that commit them to providing protection. . . .

By carefully planning their assistance with sensitivity to refugees' protection needs, NGOs can also help with the practical, on-the-ground protection of refugees. For example, if protection matters are considered when designing a refugee camp, water points, clinics and firewood-collection areas could all be located in easily accessible, well-lit areas so women and children would not have to walk long distances, alone, to make use of them.

Because of their independent status, NGOs are often the first agencies to arrive and provide assistance during an emergency. . . . NGOs can use their presence and direct involvement with individuals to help protect refugees by

- reporting protection concerns, either to government authorities and international bodies or other NGOs, as they occur;

- alerting the public and the media to those concerns;

- promoting international standards among government and local officials;

- offering legal and social advice, education and training programmes to refugees; and

- monitoring human rights both within the country of origin and within the country of asylum. . . .

United Nations High Commissioner for Refugees,
Protecting Refugees: A Field Guide for NGOs, *1999.*

Under such circumstances, insecurity and violence can plague refugee camps and settlements. Refugee women and children are particularly at risk. In their efforts to prevent and stop human rights violations, NGOs have often reported on incidents of rape and other sexual and gender-based violence or forced abductions and recruitment, problems that continue in many African and other refugee camps.

NGOs Can Assume a Vital Role

NGOs activities can thus complement and support UNHCR activities for refugees, particularly when states fail to meet their international obligations. Unlike UNHCR and states, however, NGOs do not have a protection mandate. NGOs can nevertheless be present, witness, monitor, document, report, advise, influence, and "responsibilise" states and government actors, thereby contributing to the protection and well-being of people affected by forced displacement.

Still, as was expressed at the recent UNHCR-NGO protection retreat, practical collaboration on protection in refugee situations remains uneasy. In the past, many controversies arose between UNHCR and NGOs because of a lack of dialogue or the feeling on the part of the NGOs that they were being left out of delicate debates between UNHCR and governments—debates where the NGOs' positions would and could have been supportive of UNHCR and, not least, to the refugees.

Rightly or wrongly, NGOs often have the feeling that UNHCR's policies are too submissive to the wishes of governments, instead of protecting refugees. UNHCR is a governmental agency, but it is also an agency that has a number of other stakeholders, most notably refugees and NGOs. The difficulty for the agency is that sometimes UNHCR gets caught between the contradictory desires of these stakeholders. The result is that UNHCR's policy decisions can, indeed, be troubling from the viewpoint of NGOs that are interested in pro tecting refugee rights and not states' interests. What can be more disturbing, however, is when UNHCR never engaged in a dialogue with its NGO allies to explain the rationale for its policies and decisions.

For information sharing, coordination, and cooperation on sensitive protection matters to take place effectively, UNHCR and NGOs must concentrate on developing confidence and mutual trust. Such a climate can only emerge if UNHCR and NGO staff meet on an equal footing, discuss their differences, and explore their commonalities in the protection of refugees.

> *"UNHCR [United Nations High Commissioner for Refugees] believes the rule of law is a critical factor in the delivery of effective protection to refugees, who are some of the most vulnerable people in any society."*

The UN High Commissioner for Refugees Should Be Responsible for the Refugee Problem

Thomas Albrecht

Thomas Albrecht is the deputy regional representative of the United Nations High Commissioner for Refugees (UNHCR). In the following viewpoint, Albrecht underscores the vital role UN-HCR plays in resettling and repatriating refugees, outlining their recent reforms and successes in the field.

As you read, consider the following questions:

1. What does United Nations High Commissioner for Refugees (UNHCR) believe are the most basic protections that should be afforded to refugees?

Thomas Albrecht, "Who Is Responsible for Refugee Rights," AEI.org, May 4, 2007. © 2007 American Enterprise Institute. Reproduced by permission.

2. In a UNHCR review of 82 country operations, what percentage of refugees are not able to fully enjoy freedom of movement and the right to work?

3. According to the author, how has the global refugee population changed from 2002 to 2007?

One of the refugees whose courage and strength will be in my memory forever is a woman from West Africa. Her husband was killed for political reasons by the regime in her home country. She fled with her three children to a neighboring country. Just after crossing the border she was stopped at a roadblock by rebels fighting the government in that country. She was given a terrible choice—either to stay for several days with these thugs and be sexually available as a sex slave and to cook for them, or to be turned back to persecution.

She had no choice and for the sake of her children, she stayed with the rebels. After she finally managed to move on, she was found by UNHCR [United Nations High Commissioner for Refugees] staff along the road. She thought she was safe, only to find out months later that she had been infected with HIV. After months of efforts by my UNHCR colleagues and NGO [non-governmental organization] partners to ensure her immediate protection and well-being, a resettlement country agreed to receive her and her children. She knew that she was marked for death but was consoled in the thought that her children were safe and could start life over.

This is the front line of protection. The fact that it has to be carried out more often than not in remote and dangerous locations, where a climate of impunity reigns, makes it a singularly difficult task.

Who Has Accountability?

Who is accountable for refugee rights is the topic of our discourse today. Who is accountable for the unspeakable pain and suffering of this refugee woman should be our first question, Who will hold accountable those who killed her husband and made her flee with her children? Who will hold accountable the criminals who abused her just when she thought she had reached safety? Who should answer for the reality that she could not find adequate protection in the country she fled to first?

Protecting people is one of the most important purposes and functions of the law. . . . UNHCR believes the rule of law is a critical factor in the delivery of effective protection to refugees, who are some of the most vulnerable people in any society. . . . We are of course several steps removed from this field's realities. The issues are, however, not confined to so-called developing countries. Refugee issues are often emotive ones, raising concerns over such things as state security, sovereignty and social cohesiveness. Countries express concern about perceived inequalities in the distribution of the responsibility of hosting refugees, about the growth of international crime, people smuggling and terrorism, and its alleged link to unauthorized asylum arrivals, as well as about the difficulties in trying to distinguish between refugees and migrants.

Increasingly restrictive asylum assistance in a number of countries, marked not least by the contestable interpretation of the refugee definition and barriers to accessing the asylum process, is a parallel development of growing concern. Interdiction or interception of persons, including refugees, trying to enter a country is established practice. Even while asylum in another country is still the only viable protection possibility for many of the world's forcibly displaced, the asylum space is becoming even narrower in response to security fears and local xenophobia [fear of foreigners].

Instead of the law being used as a humanitarian instrument to protect people in accordance with international obligations, it often becomes a shield to deflect those very same obligations. UNHCR's work is uncomfortable to many and even its mere existence the thorn to some.

The Role of National Governments

Who is accountable for refugee rights? As Ambassador [John] Bolton highlighted, protection of rights is fundamentally a state responsibility. This is emphasized in the 1951 convention relating to the status of refugees and the statute through which the General Assembly and the international community created UNHCR in 1950. UNHCR is a rights-based organization. Refugees and other persons of concern to us are victims of human rights abuses or human rights deficiencies and they lack a national government willing or able to redress their situation. Protection at its most basic means activities to restore rights—the right to life, the right not to suffer torture or discrimination, the right of respect for human dignity, and family unity. Protection is also about the creation of an enabling environment so that these and other rights have a real chance of being enjoyed until a durable solution is found.

These are uniquely responsibilities of states, who in addition to their legal obligations have a territory and a governance framework within which these fundamental rights can be brought to life. Freedom of religion, the right to property, the right to employment, freedom of movement, and many other rights of refugees elaborated in the Convention cannot be guaranteed by UNHCR but by states only.

UNHCR, however, frequently works with governments to encourage and support them to uphold and give meaning to basic rights of refugees. This work is critically illustrated yet again by a UNHCR review of 82 country operations, indicating that in over 50 percent of these situations, refugees are not able to fully enjoy freedom of movement and the right to work. Many are condemned to an artificial life of mercy and dependency, sometimes for a generation and more. This is neither the letter nor the spirit of the Refugee Convention, which calls for refugees to be given the same fundamental human rights that should be accorded to every human being.

To ensure that states make this obligation a reality is the core of UNHCR's mission, as difficult and almost impossible as it may be. But we also need to acknowledge the often very real limitations of countries hosting refugees who already face the challenge of realizing a meaningful existence for their own citizens. This is where UNHCR wants and needs to share accountability together with the international community. Financial support is one important measure to ensure that states can meaningfully live up to their protection obligations.

Financial Accountability Is Shared

Accountability to donors is already built into UNHCR's funding mechanism. You may be surprised to hear that virtually all contributions to UNHCR are made by states on a voluntary basis, only some 3 percent through assessed contributions. This means that UNHCR has to explain and justify each of its programs. Funding for refugee operations will only be provided if the donor is convinced of the need and the feasibility of its implementation. Through the introduction of global standards and indicators, as well as the results-based management approach, the impact of our efforts is being measured in increasing detail. Global and country reports are routinely not only provided to donors but also to the general public.

Equally important, however, is accountability to beneficiaries. So is the empowerment of refugees and the pursuit of protection and durable solutions. For some years now, UNHCR has incorporated participatory planning with refugees and partners into its program cycle. This approach has also been systematically incorporated in policies, guidelines and trainings. With regard to implementation, this increasingly means that a rights-based approach is combined with a community-based approach, or more specifically, that the concerns and priorities of the community are taken as the starting point for engaging its members in protection and programming.

However, this also means that refugees need to be part of the frequently difficult decision-making process of determining where scarce resources should be prioritized. Again, who is accountable for refugee rights, in particular where budget constraints demand choices as to which basic right should be supported more than another? How do we overcome these limitations considering that many donors have to decide among competing demands themselves to ensure that all rights can be made a reality?

Recognizing the Need for Improvement

UNHCR has long acknowledged that refugee protection is substandard in many situations. This is due, however, not only to a lack of capacity and the fact that programs to assist refugees are underfunded against the needs, but also to the insecurity prevalent in many refugee-hosting areas and the lack of freedom of movement or of self-sufficiency possibilities in closed camp environments, and the precariousness of illegal or unregularized state for urban refugees who live in marginalized communities around the towns.

Furthermore, refugee situations are still too often protracted. UNHCR and its partners have regularly reminded the international community that there are some 38 such situations worldwide. In the context in which in the late 1980s some colleagues at UNHCR have coined the term "warehouses," and this is where we are proud to jointly work with partners like Merrill Smith and the U.S. Committee for Refugees and Immigrants, in special programs in refugee-hosting countries, to engage civil society organizations in refugee protection and to advance the policy environment towards the realization of refugee rights, in particular the right to work and the freedom of movement.

Wherever possible, UNHCR works toward avoiding the use of camps and similar artificial structures. However, in some situations the setting up of camps is dictated by the circumstances, especially in large-scale emergencies, and often governments insist on the creation of camps for reasons already highlighted.

But there is also good news. In an encouraging trend, the number of refugees fell 12 percent in 2005, to 8.4 million. Over the past five years [2002–2007], the global refugee population has fallen by one-third and now stands at the lowest level since 1980. One reason for that is that over the past years we assisted large numbers of refugees to voluntarily repatriate [return to their own countries] to countries such as Afghanistan and Liberia.

To ensure and continuously improve operational efficiency and effectiveness as well as accountability, UNHCR has instituted a wide range of measures. In addition, [United Nations] High Commissioner António Guterres has committed himself and the organization to a wide-ranging reform effort, which is already bearing fruit. The time allotted is too short to elaborate on all existing oversight and accountability arrangements, so allow me to list the key aspects in some reforms.

UNHCR Reforms

In addition to the statutory obligation for the High Commissioner to frequently report to the General Assembly and the Executive Committee, the United Nations Office of Internal Oversight Services assists the Secretary General in fulfilling his internal oversight responsibilities. These arrangements are complemented by the UNHCR inspector general, who more specifically addresses the constantly evolving demands for the inspection of the quality management of UNHCR operations and headquarters units and for investigations into allegations of misconduct by UNHCR personnel. To clarify accountabilities for the staff of UNHCR as well as staff for implementing partners, the staff rules and regulations were elaborated through a code of conduct, precisely to avoid confusions . . . from the past.

Financial and management audits are routinely performed by the internal audit service and external auditors. The evaluation and policy unit is enhancing the agency's capacity for organizational learning and performance review. Evaluations are increasingly conducted jointly with personnel from governments, other international organizations and non-governmental organizations. To reinforce the impact of the evaluation function and to contribute more broadly to the enhancement of evaluation standards for humanitarian work, UNHCR is engaged in the active learning network for accountability and performance in humanitarian assistance, which brings together the evaluation specialists of many international, governmental and non-governmental organizations. All of these efforts are coupled with an ongoing dialogue with civil society.

Allow me to address in some reform one of the more particular items, as it is mentioned in the invitation, to this discussion—the issue of refugee status determination (RSD). In exceptional circumstances, UNHCR may be obliged very much by default and not by desire . . . to carry out refugee status determination in order to ensure the protection of a refugee or to pursue a special protection intervention. This again would only occur where the national authorities are either unwilling or unable to do so as well as for resettlement referrals, where resettlement countries require specific information.

Critical UNHCR Aid

While this work relates to less than 1 percent of the global refugee population, it is nevertheless of considerable importance. In 2006, refugee status determination had to be conducted in nearly 80 countries. So some 90 percent of status determination work involving some 50,000 decisions was carried out in fact in only 10 countries.

With many of these signatories, UNHCR is engaging in promoting and resourcing the transfer of refugee status deter-

The Role of UNHCR

The United Nations High Commissioner for Refugees (UNHCR), a non-political, humanitarian agency, was created by the United Nations General Assembly in December 1950 and began operations on 1 January 1951. Its mandate is to provide international protection to refugees and promote durable solutions to their problems. It does so by working with governments and, subject to the approval of the governments concerned, with private organisations. . . .

UNHCR's protection activities include:

- promoting accession to and implementation of refugee conventions and law;

- ensuring that refugees are treated in accordance with recognized international standards of law;

- ensuring that refugees are granted asylum and are not forcibly returned to the countries from which they fled;

- promoting appropriate procedures to determine whether or not a person is a refugee according to the 1951 Convention definition and to definitions found in regional conventions;

- assisting refugees in finding solutions to their problem, such as voluntary repatriation, local integration, or resettlement to a third country; and

- helping reintegrate returnees when they go home; and providing protection and assistance, when a sked to do so, to internally displaced persons.

UNHCR, "Who Is Responsible for Protecting Refugees,"
Protecting Refugees: A Field Guide, *1999.*

mination to national authorities. In some instances, governments with established RSD systems assist through training arrangements like in the case of the United States.

To support these endeavors and to provide additional oversight to field offices, in 1999 a refugee status determination unit was created in the Department of International Protection. In 2003, procedural standards for RSD under UNHCR's mandate were issued internally to set core standards and to harmonize our RSD procedures in field offices worldwide. In 2005, they were further enhanced and published. RSD training for staff and NGO partners was intensified and remains a priority, notably because of the context in which UNHCR conducts RSD. . . .

Let me say that in conclusion, I hope we can also—however, with one last word on status determination—look at the results. In the largest three operations—in Kenya, Malaysia and Egypt—the recognition rates in 2006 were between 80 and 94 percent. I hope this demonstrates, and it is also demonstrated through my presence here, that UNHCR welcomes constructive dialogue, accepts valid criticism, and admits mistakes and shortcomings. We look forward that more concerned people will join us in the difficult endeavor of ensuring the protection of refugees in good faith rather than engaging in broadside attacks that distract attention from the very people who every day demonstrate courage, perseverance and strength—the refugees who deserve our protection and our respect.

> "Wherever UNHCR [United Nations High Commissioner for Refugees] is responsible for determining refugee status, it fails to meet its own guidelines for fairness."

The UN High Commissioner for Refugees Should Have Less Responsibility for the Refugee Problem

Mauro De Lorenzo

Mauro De Lorenzo is a resident fellow at the American Enterprise Institute (AEI), a conservative think tank. In the following viewpoint, Lorenzo argues that the office of the United Nations High Commissioner for Refugees (UNHCR) has too much power and that the organization operates under little accountability and low standards. He suggests that national governments can do much better in aiding refugees and supporting them in humane and dignified conditions.

Mauro De Lorenzo, "Dignity, Safety, and Health for Refugees," washingtonpost.com, May 2, 2007. © 2007 Washingtonpost.Newsweek Interactive. Reproduced by permission of the author.

As you read, consider the following questions:

1. What do human rights lawyers Michael Alexander and Michael Kagan allege about the United Nations High Commissioner for Refugees' (UNHCR's) treatment of refugees and asylum seekers?

2. What does the author suggest as a solution to UNHCR's abuse of its power?

3. According to the author, how did UNHCR illegally punish refugees at the Kakuma camp in Kenya in 1994 and 1996?

You cannot sue the United Nations [UN]. If the UN violates your rights, that's just too bad. There is no judge with jurisdiction, no independent tribunal, no possibility of compensation or justice. A culture of impunity is built into the DNA of the UN, and some of the clearest examples can be found in the work of the United Nations High Commissioner for Refugees (UNHCR), mandated by the UN General Assembly to protect refugees around the world. Wherever UNHCR is responsible for determining refugee status, it fails to meet its own guidelines for fairness. And wherever UNHCR warehouses refugees in camps—sometimes for decades—it colludes in human rights violations on a large scale, with support from the American taxpayer.

UNHCR Is Too Powerful

In some eighty countries, UNHCR decides who is a refugee and who isn't. National governments play a secondary role, if any. In 2005, UNHCR offices received more than 88,000 applications for asylum, making it the largest refugee status decision-maker in the world. Members of the UNHCR staff conduct interviews, assess claimants' credibility, and make legal judgments about whether a claimant has a "well-founded fear of persecution." In other words, UNHCR does globally what the Department of Homeland Security [DHS] does here [in the United States].

But the decisions of DHS officers are subject to at least two levels of judicial review—not to mention legislative oversight. No one reviews UNHCR's decisions. Human rights lawyers Michael Alexander and Michael Kagan, who maintain Asylum Access's www.rsdwatch.org resource, have documented that UNHCR protection officers routinely use secret evidence against refugees, reject claims for no stated reason, fail to provide qualified interpreters, and provide no appeal system for negative decisions.

UNHCR's standard practice in the field would be laughed out of any courtroom in the United States. In fact, UNHCR's status-determination procedures fall far short of the standards that it rightly exhorts asylum authorities in Western countries to uphold. In 2005, after criticism, UNHCR simply lowered the bar for itself, issuing a new policy document that set more modest standards for its own offices than those it advocates for everyone else. But it is hardly surprising that bureaucrats who are exempt from accountability hoard their prerogatives and decline to account for their decisions.

This is serious business: When an asylum officer decides wrongly and sends a refugee back to his country of origin, the result can be imprisonment or death. Lack of accountability also means that UNHCR faces no political or legal pressure to reform and become more transparent. Though legal aid movements have successfully pressured some offices to improve, still not one UNHCR field office meets basic legal standards for fairness and due process.

Give Back Power to the States

The solution is to remove UNHCR from the equation and help national governments to determine refugee status fairly and then adjudicate decisions in their own courts. Governments botch things all the time, but it would not take much for them to do better than UNHCR. It is also a way of help-

Flaws of the United Nations System at Large

If there were ever an opportunity to look back at the original intent of those who formed UNHCR [United Nations High Commissioner for Refugees] in the wake of World War II and the refugee policies that were adopted during the Cold War—which were predominantly aimed, and I don't say this with any sense of embarrassment, at solving the legacy of the Nazi aggression in Europe and providing for refugee status for people fleeing communism in Eastern and Central Europe and the Soviet Union—here you have people fleeing the last communist dictatorship on Earth and yet somehow they seem to have trouble acquiring refugee status. . . .

I think one of the fundamental questions we have in the case of UNHCR is one that applies in a number of humanitarian situations, and that is whether the actual operation of the humanitarian situation does not in itself perpetuate the underlying political problems. So that when we look at the circumstances of large numbers of refugees who are caught in refugee camps for long periods of time—they can't be repatriated to their country of origin . . . , the country of first asylum doesn't want them, . . . and there are simply inadequate numbers of other countries that are willing to take the refugees. . . .

These camps acquire their own cultures. They are frequently used as refuges for the fighters in cases of civil strife. Everybody knows that, it's one of the worst-kept secrets in the world that we're not simply dealing with a humanitarian relief here but in effect too often rest and relaxation for fighters from various different factions. . . .

John Bolton, "Who Is Responsible for Refugee Rights"
American Enterprise Institute, May 4, 2007.

ing instill a culture of human rights in countries that often lack one. Most importantly, status determination by governments offers the possibility of judicial review of their decisions. With national governments in charge of status determination, UNHCR can be what the drafters of the 1951 Refugee Convention intended: a legal gadfly that holds governments to their obligations under international law.

Typically regarded as the paragon of humanitarianism, refugee camps are in fact one of the biggest stains on the conscience of the international community. The inmates of these facilities lack freedom of movement and have no right to work. They are sometimes not allowed to grow their own food and must depend on rations from humanitarian agencies. Those rations do not always come on time and are rarely sufficient. Refugees are forbidden to sell or barter them for other products they need, such as soap or underwear. Biological anthropologist Kenneth Porter found that Burundian adolescents born in refugee camps and raised on humanitarian assistance in Tanzania were significantly shorter than poor Tanzanian children in neighboring villages who received no assistance at all—a difference that suggests malnutrition while under international protection.

Guglielmo Verdirame of the University of Cambridge and Barbara Harrell-Bond, founding director of the Refugee Studies Center at the University of Oxford, and co-authors of *Rights in Exile: Janus-Faced Humanitarianism*, found that UNHCR in Uganda and Kenya imposed unpaid work on refugees confined to camps, supported dispute resolution mechanisms that illegally imprisoned people for adultery, and failed to protect women from genital mutilation and domestic violence.

UNHCR Violates the Geneva Convention

UNHCR has even imposed collective punishment on refugees under its protection. In the hellish Kakuma camp in northeastern Kenya, some refugees protested their conditions by destroying the enclosures through which refugees are herded to collect their food, once in April 1994 and again in April 1996. UNHCR cut off all food distribution, including to women and children, until the enclosures were rebuilt by the refugees. The suspension lasted 21 days in the first case and 14 in the second. Such measures are forbidden even in wartime by Article 33 of the Geneva Convention.

Unnecessary and inhumane, refugee camps should be replaced by forms of assistance that enable refugees to settle themselves in their host countries. Self-settlement is inconvenient for the bean counters in humanitarian organizations because it makes it more difficult to track aid distributions, and it certainly makes for less pitiful fund-raising photos. But there is no other way for a refugee to lead a dignified life in exile. An exception to the almost complete silence from international human rights organizations about the conditions in refugee camps comes from the U.S. Committee for Refugees and Immigrants, which has led a campaign against refugee warehousing since 2004, garnering bipartisan support from Senators Sam Brownback, Joe Lieberman, and Ted Kennedy. Yet UNHCR's role in planning, managing, and funding refugee camps has rarely been examined.

The United States Has the Power to Force Accountability

The United States is by far the largest donor to UNHCR. Washington provided the organization with about $330 million for 2006—almost a third of UNHCR's budget, and more than three times more than the next-largest donor. The U.S. even relies on UNHCR's deeply flawed procedures to nominate refugees for resettlement to the United States—one of the reasons that the U.S. never manages to fill the quota that Congress authorizes for refugee resettlement each year. Washington should insist on greater accountability from UNHCR.

It should assist national governments to conduct their own status determination, fund civil society groups that provide legal aid to refugees, and demand that UNHCR and host governments find alternatives to camps for dealing with long-term refugee caseloads.

It should not be much of a surprise that abuse is rampant in a system run by a professional bureaucracy that operates behind closed doors with full legal immunity. It is more surprising that human rights and refugee rights organizations hold UNHCR to such a low standard. And it is more surprising still that U.S. taxpayers should be asked to continue funding the systematic violation of refugee rights throughout the developing world.

| "The United States needs to formulate a wide-ranging and workable plan to deal with Iraq's displacement crisis."

The United States Should Do More for Iraqi Refugees

Brian Katulis and Peter Juul

Brian Katulis is a senior fellow and Peter Juul is a research associate at the Center for American Progress (CAP). In the following viewpoint, the authors state that the United States must act now to help alleviate Iraq's refugee problem by working with the Iraqi government, the United Nations, and local and international non-governmental organizations to address the problem effectively.

As you read, consider the following questions:

1. According to the United Nations High Commissioner for Refugees (UNHCR), how many Iraqis have been displaced from their homes?

2. In a recent UNHCR study, how many Iraqi refugees living in Syria plan on returning to Iraq?

3. How many Iraqi refugees are living in Syria and Jordan, according to the authors?

This Thursday [May 2008], two subcommittees of the House Foreign Affairs Committee are scheduled to hold a joint hearing on Iraq's refugee crisis. But Iraq's displaced persons crisis needs immediate action to solve the humanitarian, political, and security problems associated with it.

The United States Must Act

According to the United Nations High Commissioner for Refugees [UNHCR] 4.7 million Iraqis have so far had to leave their homes—roughly 2 million as refugees and another 2.7 million internally displaced. Yet for all the warnings of a humanitarian catastrophe that could befall Iraq if the United States redeploys its forces, little attention has been paid to Iraq's still-growing refugee crisis. Iraq's displacement crisis is not simply a moral and humanitarian problem; it represents a grave political and security challenge to Iraq and the broader Middle East. Ignoring it threatens the future stability of Iraq and the entire region. The United States must act decisively to solve, or at very least ameliorate, this problem.

Iraq's internally displaced population—not al Qaeda in Iraq or Iranian influence—is the primary threat to the country's future stability. As a recent Refugees International report demonstrated, sectarian militias—both Sunni "Concerned Local Citizens" militias and the Shi'a Mahdi Army—provide services to displaced co-religionists. Among these services is "resettling" internally displaced persons into homes that displaced members of the opposite sect have fled. This dynamic further solidifies and deepens sectarian divisions in Iraq: Neighborhoods become more homogeneous, and it makes it much more difficult for those displaced to return to their original homes. Furthermore, militias' provision of services buys loyalty and encourages revanchism among the dis-

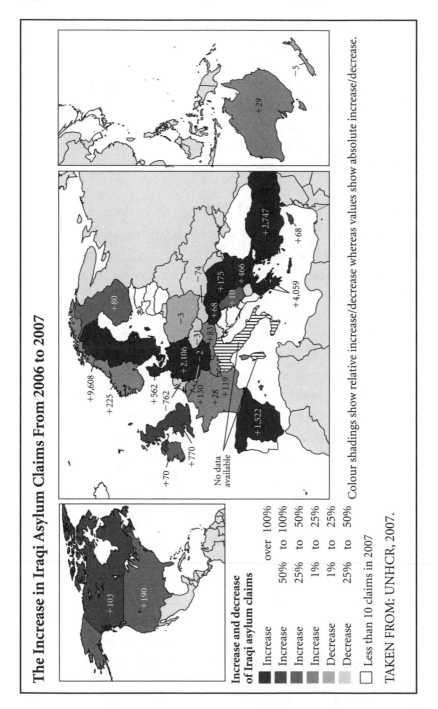

The Increase in Iraqi Asylum Claims From 2006 to 2007

Increase and decrease
of Iraqi asylum claims

Increase	over	100%
Increase	50% to	100%
Increase	25% to	50%
Increase	1% to	25%
Decrease	1% to	25%
Decrease	25% to	50%

Less than 10 claims in 2007

Colour shadings show relative increase/decrease whereas values show absolute increase/decrease.

No data available

TAKEN FROM: UNHCR, 2007.

placed. Unfortunately, neither the Iraqi government, the United States, nor the United Nations have developed workable solutions to the problem of displaced person return.

If conditions stabilize enough for their return, Iraqi refugees will face many of the same problems as the internally displaced vis-à-vis sectarian displacement and property disputes. However, the greater danger is that Iraq's refugees will become a more or less permanent stateless population that destabilizes its host countries. This danger is no idle concern: In a recent UNHCR survey of refugees in Syria, only 4 percent of those polled planned on returning to Iraq despite recent gains in security (89.5 percent said they were not planning to return to Iraq, with 6.5 percent uncertain).

Syria and Jordan are the neighboring states most affected by the Iraqi refugee crisis, with 1.2 to 1.4 million and 500,000 to 750,000 refugees respectively. Without a comprehensive solution to Iraq's internal conflict and displacement crisis, these refugees are likely to cause considerable economic, social, and political problems in their host countries that have the potential to destabilize the region.

The United States Is Not Doing Enough Now

Unfortunately, the United States is not doing nearly enough to cope with Iraq's displacement crisis. At a recent neighbors meeting in Kuwait, Secretary of State Condoleezza Rice announced that the United States' total financial contribution to Iraqi refugee assistance would top out at $278 million—less than a third of the $900 million requested by humanitarian assistance agencies. The United States has also failed to fulfill its moral responsibility to Iraqi refugees seeking to resettle elsewhere; the Swedish town of Sodertalje has resettled more Iraqi refugees (5,500) than the United States as a whole. Worse, the United States points to a trickle of refugee returns as success of its "surge" strategy without formulating a viable, comprehensive plan to resolve the issues associated with their return.

The United States needs to formulate a wide-ranging and workable plan to deal with Iraq's displacement crisis. First and foremost, the United States must work harder to resolve Iraq's multiple political conflicts that lead to violence and displacement. Equally important, the United States needs to work with the Iraqi government, the United Nations, and local and international NGOs [non-governmental organizations] to create a practical mechanism to cope with issues associated with refugee return—especially property disputes.

Advances in these two critical issues need to be made before encouraging Iraqi refugees to return *en masse* [all together]. Given the difficulty constructively addressing Iraq's conflicts and facilitating return, it is likely that Iraq's displaced will remain so for quite some time. Therefore, the United States needs to fulfill its moral responsibility and admit more Iraqi refugees into the United States for resettlement. If a country like Sweden can admit 49,000 Iraqi refugees, surely the United States can do more.

"The [United States] administration will continue to monitor the recent refugee and displacement situation and the ability of the international community to address the increased needs."

The United States Has Done a Great Deal for Iraqi Refugees

Ellen R. Sauerbrey

Ellen R. Sauerbrey was the assistant secretary of state for Population, Refugees, and Migration at the U.S. Department of State, under the President George W. Bush administration. In the following viewpoint, she outlines the generous financial assistance provided to a number of non-governmental organizations that deal directly with the Iraqi refugee crisis inside and outside of Iraq. Admitting the Iraqi refugee crisis is deepening, Sauerbrey contends that the United States will closely monitor the displacement situation and adjust funding and programs when and if needed.

Ellen R. Sauerbrey, "The Plight of the Iraqi Refugees, Statement Before the Senate Judiciary Committee, January 16, 2007," United State Committee on the Judiciary Hearings and Meetings, January 16, 2007. U.S. Department of State, Washington, DC.

As you read, consider the following questions:

1. According to Sauerbrey, how much has the U.S. government spent to support non-governmental organizations providing direct assistance to Iraqi refugees since 2003?

2. The president's fiscal year 2007 request for Migration and Refugee Assistance included how much for Iraqi humanitarian needs?

3. How is the United States expanding the resettlement program, according to Sauerbrey?

It is an honor to appear before you today [January 16, 2007] to discuss issues involving displaced Iraqis and Iraqi refugees. I welcome the opportunity to detail some of the actions the [George W. Bush] administration is taking to provide protection and assistance for Iraqis in neighboring countries of first asylum and for populations inside Iraq. The administration shares your concern about the current situation facing Iraqi refugees and is committed to helping improve conditions for them in countries of first asylum. We are working closely with host governments in the region, the United Nations High Commissioner for Refugees (UNHCR), the International Committee of the Red Cross (ICRC), and non-governmental organizations (NGOs). Through these partners, we are providing assistance to the most needy refugees and are seeking durable solutions, including resettlement to the United States, for those who require this important form of international protection.

Since 2003, the administration has provided more than $800 million to support WFP [United Nations World Food Programme], UNHCR, ICRC, the International Organization for Migration [IOM], and a range of NGOs that provide direct assistance to returning Iraqi refugees, internally displaced persons (IDPs) in Iraq, and third country national refugees inside Iraq and Iraqi refugees outside Iraq to help meet basic humanitarian needs and support reintegration programs. U.S. government support has increased the capacity of Iraqi government ministries working with refugees and internally displaced persons, provided training to non-governmental organizations serving refugees, and assisted numerous victims of conflict. These programs helped reintegrate many of the 300,000 Iraqi refugees who returned home between 2003 and 2006 and helped many of the 500,000 IDPs inside Iraq.

There Is a Growing Refugee Problem

However, due to the upsurge in sectarian violence in 2006, this trend has reversed, and at present, more Iraqis are fleeing their homes to other areas of Iraq and to neighboring countries than are returning. UNHCR estimates that between 1 to 1.4 million Iraqis are in countries bordering Iraq, though a large percentage of them had left Iraq prior to 2003. We believe the current population of Iraqis in Jordan and Syria is a mixture of the Iraqis who departed before 2003 and newer arrivals. Many organizations, including UNHCR, have raised concerns about new arrivals and growing numbers of Iraqis in these countries, though neither UNHCR nor the governments of Jordan or Syria have definitive figures on the size of the population. UNHCR has argued that the refugee crisis it predicted would occur, but did not materialize after the invasion in 2003, is now upon us.

Although we lack firm figures on how many Iraqis are seeking refuge in neighboring countries we do know that many left with minimal resources and are living on the margins. Other than Al-Ruwaished, which shelters a stable population of third country nationals from Iraq, Jordan and UNHCR have not established refugee camps. Anecdotal reporting also indicates that many Iraqi children in these countries do not have access to schools or adequate health care. We need better information on the needs of Iraqis in these countries, particularly their protection concerns. We are encouraging the government of Jordan to allow a comprehensive survey of the needs of Iraqis in Jordan that would guide the international community in focusing assistance and protection activities. UNHCR is planning to conduct a similar survey in Syria. We hope our partners will be able to complete these surveys in the very near future.

The United States Has Responded Adequately

However, we are not waiting for precise numbers before responding to the needs of vulnerable Iraqis in neighboring countries. Rather, we are continuing our support to UNHCR and NGO programs benefiting Iraqis in these countries. In 2006, the U.S. provided nearly $8 million of UNHCR's operational budget for Iraq, Jordan, Syria, and Lebanon. In 2006, we also provided $3.3 million in funding to the International Catholic Migration Commission to assist the most vulnerable Iraqis in Lebanon, Syria and Jordan. In 2007, we are expanding support for these and similar programs serving needy Iraqis in neighboring countries. But our ability to respond to the growing needs depends on receiving sufficient resources. The president's FY [fiscal year] 2007 request for Migration and Refugee Assistance included $20 million for Iraqi humanitarian needs. The administration will continue to monitor the recent refugee and displacement situation and the ability of the international community to address the increased needs.

Our support for UNHCR's protection mandate and our diplomatic efforts with host governments is essential to preserve the principle of first asylum and ensure that assistance reaches vulnerable refugees. We continue to press all governments in the region to keep their borders open to those with a fear of persecution and allow assistance and protection to reach these populations. Jordan and Syria have been generous hosts to Iraqis for many years, and have largely kept their borders open as people continued to flow out of Iraq in 2006.

Iraqi Refugees in the United States, 2009

The United States expects to admit a minimum of 17,000 Iraqi refugees in fiscal 2009, which begins October 1 [2008], the department's senior coordinator for refugees said. Thousands more Iraqis and their family members could arrive through a special visa program for people who worked for the United States or its contractors.

Susan Cornwell,
"Tens of Thousands of Iraqis May Come to U.S. in '09,"
Reuters, September 12, 2008.

Both Jordan and Syria are also hosts to sizeable Palestinian refugee populations, and we recognize the additional burden Iraqi refugees place on these countries. We are working with UNHCR and host governments to see how we can help bolster their capacity to provide protection and assistance so Iraqis do not overstretch social service networks and these governments' ability to continue to receive Iraqis seeking asylum.

U.S. Resettlement Program Plays a Key Role

Another aspect of our response to Iraqi refugee needs in the region is a planned expansion of our U.S. resettlement program. Given the large numbers of Iraqis thought to be in Syria and Jordan, with some estimates as high as 1.4 million, the U.S. and other third country resettlement programs will play a small but important role in meeting the needs of Iraqi refugees. For that reason, we are working closely with UNHCR to prioritize U.S. resettlement for the most vulnerable Iraqi refugees. The U.S. has been resettling Iraqi refugees since the mid-1970s. To date the U.S. has resettled more than 37,000

Iraqis, the vast majority of whom were victims of Saddam Hussein's regime. As the numbers of Iraqis arriving in Jordan and Syria increased in 2006, we have acted aggressively to expand our ability or offer more Iraqis refuge in the United States. In 2006, we provided $400,000 of funding targeted to support UNHCR resettlement operations. These expanded operations will increase registration efforts to help identify vulnerable cases and boost the number of referrals to our program and those of other resettlement countries. We have provided an additional $500,000 for this purpose in 2007. We have no quota on the number of Iraqis who can be resettled to the United States as refugees. The process of resettling Iraqis is the same as resettling refugees in need of protection from other parts of the world. This process includes identifying those in greatest need from among so many, conducting adequate background security checks, completing personal interviews with adjudications, and coordinating the transportation and logistics for individuals approved for resettlement. In processing eligible Iraqis for resettlement in the United States, we will remain vigilant in preventing terrorists from gaining admission to this country.

I want to recognize some of the special populations that have received notice from humanitarian organizations in 2006—minority populations in Iraq and Iraqis who have worked closely with the United States in Iraq. Some have called for special protection and programs for these people, including religious minorities such as Christians, who have fled Iraq or those who have worked for the American government or U.S. organizations or companies. Many of these Iraqis are in refuge in Jordan, Syria, or Turkey and may be unable to return to Iraq because they fear for their lives. We intend to ensure that these special populations receive the same consideration and access to the U.S. resettlement program as others and we are encouraging them to contact UNHCR to make their needs known.

Description of Programs Inside Iraq

I want to take a moment to talk about important programs the U.S. government supports inside Iraq. While recent reports have highlighted the conditions of Iraqis in neighboring countries, we must not forget populations of concern still inside Iraq. UNHCR and the Iraqi government estimate there are as many as 1.7 million internally displaced persons and another 44,082 third country national refugees in Iraq. The U.S. government continues to support UNHCR, ICRC, and key NGO programs inside the country that assist communities with new internally displaced persons, recently returned refugees, and other victims of violence. For example, we support important programs of ICRC that upgrade hospitals throughout the country and provide medical services to those who are innocent victims of the armed insurgency. We also provide resources and diplomatic support to programs that seek to protect, assist, and provide durable solutions for Palestinian, Turkish, and Iranian refugees inside Iraq. In 2005 and 2006, we supported the movement of over 3,000 Iranian Kurdish refugees from the al Tash refugee camp near the strife-tom town of al Ramadi to a safe area in Northern Iraq—providing permanent housing, employment programs, and local integration support. We are also working closely with UNHCR and the governments of Iraq and Turkey to enable the voluntary return of more than 10,000 Turkish Kurdish refugees from the Mahlanour refugee camp to their home villages in Turkey.

The U.S. Agency for International Development continues to support the protection and assistance requirements of internally displaced persons (IDPs) in Iraq, mostly through non-governmental organizations. These NGOs work closely with new IDPs to provide life-saving and sustainable assistance throughout the country. The administration will continue to implement existing programs and monitor the displacement situation.

Periodical Bibliography

Morton Abramowitz, George Rupp, John Whitehead, and James Wolfensohn — "A Surge for Refugees," *The New York Times*, April 22, 2008.

Daniel Byman — "Iraqi's Displacement Crisis and the International Response," Center for American Progress, February 11, 2008.

Daniel Byman — "The Next Phase of the Iraqi War: Why We Must Welcome Thousands of Iraqi Refugees to the United States," Slate.com, November 15, 2007.

Roger Cohen — "Refugees? What Refugees?" *The New York Times*, September 27, 2007.

Ivan Eland — "A Responsibility to Help Iraqi Refugees," IntellectualConservative.com, June 12, 2007.

Michael Gershon — "Another Test in Iraq: Our Aid to Refugees," *The Washington Post*, August 22, 2007.

Joe Guzzardi — "Refugee Status for Iraqi Translators? Let's Look at the Big Picture," VDARE.com, March 23, 2007.

Anna Husarka — "With Iraqi Refugees in Jordan," Slate.com, February 8, 2007.

Edward M. Kennedy — "We Can't Ignore Iraq's Refugees," *The Washington Post*, December 30, 2006.

Andrew Lam — "Iraqi Refugees Find No Haven in US," *The Nation*, January 23, 2007.

John Ross — "One More Cruel Hoax: Iraqi Refugees Return," *Counterpunch*, December 14, 2007.

Anne-Marie Slaughter — "Remember the Refugees," *The New York Times*, May 4, 2008.

What U.S. Policies Can Help Alleviate the Refugee Problem?

Chapter Preface

After the terrorist attacks on September 11, 2001, the United States began to scrutinize its immigration policies to better protect itself and its citizens from potential terrorists finding their way into the country. To tighten restrictions on refugees and immigrants crossing the borders, the U.S. Congress passed the USA PATRIOT Act in October 2001 and the REAL ID Act of 2005. The provisions of these acts broaden the scope of what is known as the "material support bar," which blocks the entrance into the United States of any refugee who has provided material support to any known terrorist organization.

The Patriot Act and REAL ID Act also broaden the definition of "terrorist activity" and "terrorist organization," which in effect renders any refugee ineligible for entry into the United States if he or she has committed "an act that the actor knows, or reasonably should know, affords material support (1) for the commission of a terrorist act; (2) to any individual who the actor knows, or reasonably should know, has committed or plans to commit a terrorist activity or (3) to a designated or non-designated terrorist organization.;" As a result of these changes, the "material support bar" has proven to be one of the most controversial immigration laws in recent memory.

Under the current broad definitions of "material support" and "terrorist organization," a vast number of refugees once eligible for entrance into the United States is now ineligible— including, some critics of the policy assert, refugees who are truly at risk and need help from the United States. For example, according to the Department of Homeland Security, an asylum seeker who supported Afghanistan's Northern Alliance in the 1990s would be barred from entering the United States even though the Northern Alliance was fighting the Taliban government, a regime the U.S. government considered illegitimate.

There is a waiver provision that would allow the U.S. government to resettle refugees who have provided material support to certain groups out of necessity. It is rarely used, however.

The function and effect of the material support bar is one of the issues discussed in the following chapter, which focuses on U.S. policies that address the refugee problem. Other viewpoints explore the policy of increasing developmental aid, and debate adjusting the number of refugees that enter the United States every year.

"The stories of refugees today have echoes in many stories of the founding and growth of our nation."

U.S. Immigration Policy Is Working Correctly

Ellen R. Sauerbrey

Ellen R. Sauerbrey was assistant secretary of state for Population, Refugees, and Migration at the U.S. Department of State, under the President George W. Bush administration. In the following viewpoint, she conveys a sense of a refugee's plight and delineates how the United States works to alleviate the refugee problem, focusing on specific actions the U.S. government has taken to improve the lives of refugees all over the world.

As you read, consider the following questions:

1. What is one of the things Sauerbrey lists that the U.S. government funds at the Kakuma Camp in Kenya?

2. How many Afghani refugees were able to return home by 2006, according to the author?

3. According to Sauerbrey, how many refugees from how many countries did the United States accept in 2005?

Ellen R. Sauerbrey, "The U.S. Commitment to Refugee Protection and Assistance: A Humanitarian and Strategic Imperative," Heritage Lecture 951, June 20, 2006. Copyright © 2006 The Heritage Foundation. Reproduced by permission.

You have escaped alive. Your life will not be what it was, but your life will continue. You can't go back to where they deny you your rights, where they take your possessions, where they hurt you and your family, where they may even try to kill you because of who you are—because of your faith, your political stance, your ethnic background, your social group.

You are among the approximately 13 million human beings in our world today who are in this situation. You are the Karen villagers driven out by the oppressive rulers of Burma; the religious minorities of Iran; the victims of violence in Darfur; the North Koreans, subject to imprisonment or torture for the crime of escaping and seeking a better life. You are among the ethnic Nepali, expelled from Bhutan in an act of ethnic cleansing.

Now, you are in a camp or a shelter. You are subject to the good graces of your hosts, waiting for the day when you can go home again—if things change at home, or if you are offered a permanent status in your country of refuge, or if you are resettled to another land. But you are hoping for a better future. What difference does your plight make to anyone in the United States? What difference does it make to the government of the United States?

We as Americans want to help.

America Is a Land of Refugees

As individuals, we respond with empathy and concern. Those of us so blessed as to have been born and raised in the United States, and who have lived our lives in freedom, can only imagine the plight of refugees. Even so, maybe your parents or your grandparents fled to this country, seeking opportunity or escaping oppression in the lands of their birth. The stories of refugees today have echoes in many stories of the founding and growth of our nation. And the welcoming response of the United States is famously summarized in the stirring words

121

Refugee Arrivals by Country of Nationality

Country	2007		2006		2005	
	Number	Percent	Number	Percent	Number	Percent
Total	48,217	100.0	41,150	100.0	53,738	100.0
Burma	13,896	28.8	1,612	3.9	1,447	2.7
Somalia	6,969	14.5	10,357	25.2	10,405	19.4
Iran	5,481	11.4	2,792	6.8	1,856	3.5
Burundi	4,545	9.4	466	1.1	214	0.4
Cuba	2,922	6.1	3,143	7.6	6,360	11.8
Russia	1,773	3.7	6,003	14.6	5,982	11.1
Iraq	1,608	3.3	202	0.5	198	0.4
Liberia	1,606	3.3	2,402	5.8	4,289	8.0
Ukraine	1,605	3.3	2,483	6.0	2,889	5.4
Vietnam	1,500	3.1	3,039	7.4	2,009	3.7
Other	6,312	13.1	8,651	21.0	18,089	33.7

TAKEN FROM: U.S. Department of State, Bureau of Population, Refugees, and Migration (PRM), Worldwide Refugee Admissions Processing System (WRAPS).

inscribed on the Statue of Liberty, words written by Emma Lazarus, a descendant of European Jews who fled religious persecution. You have all heard them: "Give me your tired . . . your huddled masses, yearning to breathe free."

This history, compassion, and dedication to upholding human dignity make up our humanitarian imperative. This is why collectively as a nation we continue to concern ourselves with the plight of refugees. I'm honored that President George W. Bush and Secretary of State Condoleezza Rice have charged me with the responsibility of reflecting the best humanitarian traditions of the American people and with providing, with taxpayers' money, protection and life-sustaining relief for refugees and victims of conflict around the world.

According to the definition of the United Nations [UN] Convention on Refugees, which we have largely adopted as U.S. law, a refugee is a person who is outside of his or her home country, and who cannot return due to a well-founded fear of persecution based on race, religion, nationality, political origin, or membership in a particular group. So, as we talk about refugees, remember that we are not talking about people who are trying to arrive in our country seeking a better economic future. We are talking about people who are victims of tyranny, oppression, and persecution.

The Office of the [United Nations] High Commissioner for Refugees, or UNHCR, also concerns itself with other vulnerable persons, including internally displaced persons, or IDPs. They have the same needs as refugees; the difference is that while IDPs have escaped from a conflict or a humanitarian crisis of some kind, they are still within their own country. In our hemisphere, Colombia, for example, has one of the largest concentrations of IDPs who have fled from the attacks on their villages by the Revolutionary Armed Forces of Colombia. Working with international partners, we have made life better for millions of refugees and internally displaced persons that live in far-flung refugee camps.

The U.S. Commitment

I had the opportunity in the spring [of 2006] to visit one of these camps, the Kakuma Camp in Kenya. And there I was able to see the benefit of the work that we do through not only an international organization like UNHCR, but also through non-governmental organizations (NGOs) like the International Rescue Committee. I saw a number of things that we fund: latrines that help with sanitation to reduce cholera, mosquito nets, a 120-bed hospital. I saw a physical therapist working on the legs of a tiny, tiny infant who had been born with cerebral palsy. I saw the therapeutic feeding of children who were in danger of dying of malnutrition. We are sustaining life as well by helping fund the World Food Programme, whose food aid prevents food supply interruptions in refugee camps.

We also fund health and sanitation projects in Chad, where so many of the victims who have fled Darfur are located. One of our projects, designed by an American NGO, and again, this happens to be the International Rescue Committee, pipes water into the camp, right on the edge of the desert in Chad. By bringing the water into the camp, this project prevents further human rights abuses. Women no longer have to go out of the camp to collect water, where they may be subject to rape and other violence.

We are also preventing and addressing sexual abuse and exploitation—a terrible problem for the most vulnerable populations—by insisting on higher standards of performance from our partners. Our implementing partners have to sign a code of conduct. We fund training to develop respect for the human rights and dignity of all people, especially women, and we are empowering victims, through, for example, legal advocacy programs that enable women in West Africa to prosecute their abusers. This is so important to breaking the culture of impunity that allows the abuses in the first place.

Education and Self-Sufficiency

We are also focused on the need for education, and we have funded schools all over the world. For Afghan refugees in Pakistan, for example, these schools are providing opportunities and hope for the future, particularly for girls. We fund education projects on democracy, human rights, and tolerance that reach half a million Palestinian refugee children.

Self-sufficiency is something that we Americans believe in very strongly. To help refugees become self-sufficient, we support vocational training and economic opportunities. When I was in Kakuma Camp, I had the opportunity to visit programs where I saw equal numbers of men and women learning to sew, learning auto mechanics, learning construction trades, and being prepared for the day when they can go home again, when they will have a marketable skill.

Now, these are the kinds of things that we do "in camps," and that assistance is substantial. But our major goal is to provide durable solutions for refugees, many of whom have been in camps for decades. In too many cases, babies are born and reach maturity without ever knowing anything except life in a refugee camp.

Refugees Aim to Go Home

It is true that most refugees want to go home. That's a natural human instinct. And indeed, they are returning home in unprecedented numbers to places like Afghanistan, where 4.5 million have already [by the summer of 2006] returned home—one of the great success stories of our time. Many other refugees have returned to Iraq, Liberia, Burundi, and Southern Sudan. All of them are former victims of conflict, terror, and tyranny, and they are now home, rebuilding their lives and rebuilding their countries.

We have supported repatriation in safety and dignity for many of these populations. The Afghan story is already one of the most wonderful humanitarian success stories we can claim.

But we also look to Liberia, where large numbers of Liberians are returning home. Sustaining these returns is an important part of this process. It does no good to send people back if they turn around because there is nothing there for them, and they return to refugee camps. Sustaining returns will continue to test and strengthen our country's commitment to help people build new lives in freedom.

Sometimes, refugees are able to make new lives in the country in which they have found refuge, and again, our diplomacy seeks to encourage self-reliance and local integration. But many of the countries of first asylum are themselves troubled countries with few resources, and they are to be commended for their generosity and sacrifice in hosting large refugee populations. For example, Pakistan at one point in time was hosting these millions of Afghanistan refugees who are now going home. Tanzania today hosts over 500,000 refugees.

Often, host countries are not able to integrate refugee populations and the refugees do not have an option of going home. There is no option but resettlement in another country that has the means and the willingness to offer refugees a new start in life. The United States has a proud record of assisting refugees in many such nations, as well as offering many refugees a chance for a new life, a new home, a new start in America. Since World War II, more refugees have found permanent homes in the United States than in any other country. This past year [2005] we opened our doors to 53,000 refugees from 55 different countries. This is more than all of the other resettlement countries in the world combined. To put this in perspective, since 1975 the United States has resettled more than 2.6 million refugees.

"As lawmakers translated raw fear into clumsy statutes, some would-be Americans suffered in ways the numbers do not convey."

U.S. Immigration Policy Has Made It Too Difficult for Refugees to Enter the Country

Kerry Howley

Kerry Howley is a senior editor at Reason *and Reason.com. In the following viewpoint, she observes that for the past several years, increasingly draconian immigration laws, including the material support bar for refugees, have had a negative economic impact on the United States.*

As you read, consider the following questions:

1. According to Howley, how many immigrant visas did the United States issue in 2001 and 2005?

2. What does the author feel is the reason the United States issues too few refugee and immigrant visas?

Kerry Howley, "Bad Fences Make Bad Neighbors: How 9/11 Dumbed Down the Immigration Debate," *Reason*, September 11, 2006. Copyright © 2006 by Reason Foundation, 3415 S. Sepulveda Blvd., Suite 400, Los Angeles, CA 90034. www.reason.com. Reproduced by permission.

3. According to a 2004 study, immigration delays cost American businesses how much money?

At the beginning of September 2001, immigration was much in the news. President [George W.] Bush wanted to legalize more Mexicans who were working in America without documentation, and [Representative] Tom Tancredo was loudly opposed. Business leaders said immigrants would bring economic growth; [conservative political activist] Phyllis Schlafly said they would bring tuberculosis. *Amnesty* was a dirty word. [Senator] Joseph Lieberman told *The New York Times*, "Fences are going to go down between these two countries." Republican conservatives opposed legalization, and President Bush started to hedge.

9/11 Changed the Immigration Debate

How drastically has the situation changed since then? According to the Department of Homeland Security, the U.S. issued 406,080 immigrant visas in 2001 and 395,005 in 2005. The country admitted too few legal immigrants in 2005, just as it did in 2001, and 9/11 [2001 terrorist attacks] seems to have had little lasting effect. Terror's major contribution was to end talk of legalization until Bush resurrected the issue in 2004.

Of course, the [9/11 airplane] hijackers weren't immigrants at all. They were visitors carrying temporary visas. And since September 2001, America has been far more suspicious of visitors who come to study, sightsee, or strike a deal. Americans hardly felt the transition that killed the Immigration and Naturalization Service (INS), but foreigners endured longer waits and more rejections as the number of visas issued dropped precipitously. Virtually every visa application now requires an interview, and applicants can wait months to score one. Certain groups, such as foreign science students and visitors traveling from Arab countries, are subject to more bureaucracy and longer waits. Immigration courts have been havens of secrecy; even immigration lawyers complain they really

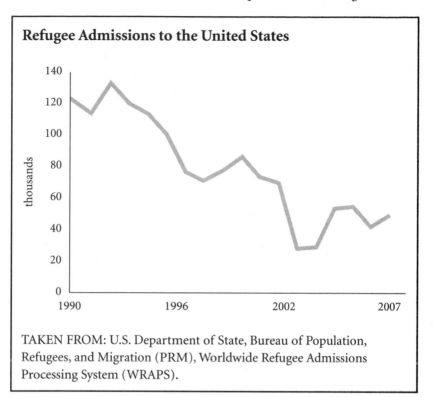

Refugee Admissions to the United States

TAKEN FROM: U.S. Department of State, Bureau of Population, Refugees, and Migration (PRM), Worldwide Refugee Admissions Processing System (WRAPS).

don't understand the process. A 2004 survey by industry groups found visa delays cost American businesses $30 billion between July 2002 and March 2004.

As lawmakers translated raw fear into clumsy statutes, some would-be Americans suffered in ways the numbers do not convey. The U.S. has long been generous to refugees, but a provision of the [USA] PATRIOT Act has kept thousands of refugees from resettlement in the United States. The act denies asylum to those who have given "material support" to terrorists, even under duress, while a provision of the REAL ID Act expands the definition of *terrorist*. Myanmar refugees forced to share a meal with rebels (who are fighting a government at least as terror-driven as they are) and Colombians who surrendered possessions to armed, guerilla groups are regularly turned away.

We Need Immigrants and Refugees

Still, temporary visa issuances have been creeping back up. The necessities of international capitalism are too pressing for such restrictions to endure. The State Department is trying to increase staffing at foreign consulates, and a sharp, extended drop in foreign students shows signs of leveling off.

The conversation has returned to immigration from Mexico, and the debate is almost the same one that was going on before the [World Trade Center] towers fell. How have the terms changed? Those who support open borders make the same arguments they've been making for decades, but the Tom Tancredos [a former Republican representative and adamant opposer of illegal immigration] of the world now counter with the lexicon of terror. Just as Iraqis and Saudis somehow became indistinguishable in the rhetorical aftermath of 9/11, Middle Eastern terrorists who come by air are conflated with Mexicans who come on foot. The skies are calm, but the desert teems with invaders. Immigrants are no longer poor people looking for jobs, or even unapologetic lawbreakers, but living symbols of the holes they slipped through.

We didn't have a plan for immigration reform then, and we don't have one now. The shift is conceptual, captured in language if not in law. When Joe Lieberman told *The New York Times* that "fences are going to go down between these two countries," he was expressing a mainstream political position. The most illuminating part of this sentiment is not the hope Lieberman expressed but the cliché he chose to express it. Back in 2001, after all, the word *fence* was just a metaphor.

> "In the wake of 9/11 [2001 terrorist at-
> tacks], there would be considerable
> popular support for an admissions
> cap—if it were to be openly and hon-
> estly debated."

The United States Should Limit the Number of Refugees Entering the Country

Thomas Allen

Thomas Allen is a contributor to VDARE.com, a Webzine that advocates reduced immigration. In the following essay, he asserts that the United States should pass legislation to institute a cap on the number of refugees admitted into the country every year, which would result in more resources for refugee assistance overseas.

As you read, consider the following questions:

1. Why has Jewish refugee migration from the former Soviet Union to the United States dropped off dramatically
   in recent years, according to the author?

2. How many refugees does the author believe should be
   admitted to the United States under a legislated cap?

3. Why does the author believe that the time is right to openly and honestly discuss the possibility of capping refugee admissions to the United States?

The town around the United Nations' [UN's] Kakuma refugee camp in Kenya—staging ground for the current controversial importation of Somali Bantu into Middle America—grew from 5,000 in 1990 to 40,000 in 2000. Kenyans from other parts of the country moved in to take advantage of social services, jobs and trading opportunities that sprang up around the UN camp.

So dependent on UN refugee camps are some areas in Kenya that local residents staged demonstrations [in 2002] to protest closure of one of them.

Worldwide, the UN has officially recognized about 12 million people as "refugees." They may well finish up here. Since 1992, over three-quarters (77%) of the UN-recognized refugees who were resettled permanently in industrialized countries came to the U.S.

The Refugee Industry

And, as in Kenya, a refugee industry has grown up here in the U.S. It forms an "Iron Triangle" exactly like the Civil Rights Industry's iron triangle that Hugh Graham described in *Collision Course*, his pathbreaking study of the "convergence of affirmative action and immigration policy in America": 1) interest group; 2) Congressional Committee; 3) federal agency.

The refugee Iron Triangle is also aided by a lawyer lobby—and a media which is seemingly incapable of reporting truthfully on the issue.

The Refugee Industry as we know it would end tomorrow if even one quarter of refugee costs were the responsibility of its champions.

The largest such champion: the Roman Catholic Church. As the Acton Institute's Father Robert A. Sirico has demonstrated, Catholic charities have become addicted to federal money. Money is fungible. Because the taxpayer pays many of the bills for its social vision, the Catholic Church has funds to spend on political advocacy—and $1 billion in hush money to cover up a decades-long sex scandal. (I am afraid President [George W.] Bush's Faith Based Initiative will only expand this dysfunctional model.)

The second-largest refugee resettlement contractor, in terms of refugees recently resettled in the U.S.: the Hebrew Immigrant Aid Society (HIAS).

Jewish Refugee Immigration

Jewish refugee immigration from the former Soviet Union [FSU] to the U.S. has fallen off dramatically in recent years. An incredible 500,000 Jews have come here since the 1980s. But now the FSU is simply running out of Jews. Also important, Jews leaving the FSU are now being directed to Israel, instead of their preferred destinations in the West. They are needed for Israel's demographic policy.

The [Jewish newspaper] *Forward* reports that

> Jewish immigration agencies such as the New York Association for New Americans have seen their refugee budgets halved in the past three years alone, while the Hebrew Immigrant Aid Society has openly debated what role Jewish immigration agencies should play in an era without large numbers of Jewish immigrants.

So what "role" does the Hebrew Immigrant Aid Society decide to play? *It opens a satellite office in Nairobi Kenya— where it will most certainly be facilitating African Muslim refugee Immigration to the U.S.* (About 50% of today's UNHCR [United Nations High Commissioner for Refugees] refugees are from Muslim countries, not including Palestinians who are counted on the books of another UN refugee agency, UNRWA [UN Relief Works Agency for Palestine Refugees in the Near East].)

This may seem paradoxical, given Jewish concerns about the growing Muslim population in the U.S. But Leonard Glickman, president and CEO of HIAS and formerly a spokesman for the U.S. Federal Office of Refugee Resettlement, told the *Forward*'s [Nacha] Cattan, "The more diverse American society is the safer [Jews] are."

Refugee admissions to the U.S. declined sharply in 2002 as a result of 9/11 [2001 terrorist attacks]. But most experts expect this decline will be temporary. A suggestion to temporarily "re-program" federal money from domestic resettlement agencies to refugee assistance programs overseas—where funds are quite literally hundreds of times more effective—was angrily denounced by those resettlement contractors at a January 2002 meeting with State Department officials.

The State Department capitulated. It kept funding at the previous year's level—even though the contractors were dealing with less than half the refugee caseload.

Additionally, State agreed to allow the refugee contractors a more influential role in picking refugees for admission to the U.S.

Make that an Iron Triangle of interest group, Congressional Committee and *weak* federal agency.

A Political and Financial Controversy

Remember this when advocates for higher refugee admissions start talking about the "indivisibility of humankind" or of refugees as a "borderless" problem—and thus a matter of collective international responsibility.

These American refugee advocates chose to steal the paltry food rations from overseas refugee camps to preserve their cushy [Washington] D.C. jobs.

The Refugee Industry has also spawned a new academic discipline, "Refugee Studies." Some of its ideologists are demanding an international "rights-based regime," under which individuals officially designated as refugees by the UN would never be confined to a camp, but automatically allowed to settle wherever they wish.

This may seem a distant dream today. But there is serious discussion about creating an international clearinghouse which assigns refugees more or less automatically to host countries based on a formula which weighs host country GDP [gross domestic product], population density and other measures of stability and wealth.

The more successful the country, the larger will be its per capita refugee quota.

Guess what that means?

This is not to minimize the suffering of refugees. Nor to say the U.S. should not participate in helping find solutions.

But the U.S. is already the largest single contributor to UN refugee work. It pays about a quarter of the budget for the UNHCR and UNRWA.

And the U.S. could fully fund 10 UNHCRs with what it spends on resettlement of refugees in the U.S., including their ongoing welfare costs.

Cap Refugee Admissions

Personally, I can accept that it might be appropriate to resettle some refugees in America. But before any New World Order refugee resettlement regime takes form, the U.S. should revisit legislation capping refugee admissions.

Currently, the refugee quota is set each year by the administration in consultation with Congress and various interest groups. It is a tempting prize to hand out in exchange for political support.

A legislated cap, say to 25,000 a year, would reduce the value of the quota as a political tool. It would also free up more resources for refugee assistance overseas.

Granted, overseas aid too can be politicized, as can the very designation of who the U.S. should regard as a "refugee."

The Refugee Image in the Media

The media image of the refugee continues to be women and children staggering to the sanctuary here with a few worldly possessions on their backs, pursued by knout-wielding Cossacks [Russians who used to whip criminals]. In fact, of course, the net effect of the 1980 Refugee Act has been to create a special type of expedited, subsidized immigration for politically favored groups, regardless of any objective need. In the U.S., a veritable NGO [non-governmental organization] Nation of at least 400 federal government-dependent refugee agencies and affiliates has grown up on the basis of welfare as we knew it, a gullible media, dubious accounting practices and the entry of refugees into the ranks of salaried service providers and lobbyists for future waves of refugees. Perhaps an additional 400 smaller exclusive ethnic organizations and spin-offs are supported by state and local governments. This Refugee Industry is dedicated to bringing in more "refugees"—often brazenly presenting their case before Congress in terms of the employment it provides for Americans, a.k.a. themselves.

Thomas Allen,
"Refugee Industry Shows the Media—For Now,"
VDARE.com, July 31, 2002.

But at least overseas refugee programs would not result in the displacement and dispossession of Americans in their own hometowns.

An admissions cap was considered at the time of the original 1980 Refugee Act. The idea has been discussed from time to time since then. This may be the last chance. U.S. foreign policy increasingly converges with the global human rights agenda—part of which has always called for a permanent high-volume flow of refugees to the West.

In the wake of 9/11, there would be considerable popular support for an admissions cap—if it were to be openly and honestly debated.

We know who would oppose any such debate—and now we know why.

> *"Give a woman a fish, you've fed her for one day; give her a fishing pole—she can sell the damn thing and buy something that she really needed, but you wouldn't have known if you didn't ask."*

Increasing Development Assistance Can Help Solve the Refugee Problem

Merrill Smith

Merrill Smith is the editor of World Refugee Survey *for the U.S. Committee for Refugees and Immigrants (USCRI). In the following viewpoint, Smith notes that there is an institutionalized dependence on humanitarian assistance to refugees and urges greater development assistance, which will provide long-term, durable solutions to the refugee problem.*

As you read, consider the following questions:

1. Why does the author believe that there is such an emphasis on humanitarian assistance and not on development assistance?

2. How does Smith describe the Millennium Challenge Account (MCA)?

3. Where does the author believe that the MCA failed?

First I will have to note, although this may be a little boring, the consensus that seems to be pretty well established that I don't think was really always there. There's widespread agreement now that warehousing is wrong. As has been noted, we are not the first persons to use the term. In our 2004 survey, where we launched a campaign to end the warehousing of refugees, I put a major article up, of which copies are there. You'll indeed note in the footnotes that many of the sources are UNHCR [United Nations High Commissioner for Refugees] sources. Certainly did not have an original thought there, but I certainly wanted to collect it and put it before a public audience.

Ending Warehousing

But if you will give real credit to someone for the campaign to end the warehousing of refugees, the aims of which all seem to be endorsed here, I think it would have to go to the founders of the 1951 Convention. They are the ones who when pressed with massive refugee flows in Europe, many in camps, could have done a lot of things when they drafted that convention. But they drafted a convention that not only defined a refugee and enshrined the principle of non-refoulement, but it spelled out a virtual bill of rights for refugees, which we like to highlight in that article as the anti-warehousing rights of the 1951 Convention, including the right to work, to freedom of movement, to practice professions. To essentially—to sum it up in one phrase—to live as normal a life as possible even while awaiting a durable solution.

The word "camp" does not appear once in the 1951 Convention. We checked. We were looking for rules about how far a camp can be from a border, looking for the standards now in the Spearer [phonetic] standards, but it wasn't there. They didn't mention it, which is odd because today we think of refugee camps—camps are for refugees, refugees belong in camps. It's almost one word.

Also the Convention doesn't mention the expression we know today as "durable solutions." It does mention the solutions—citizenship in the host country, reinstallation in the source country—not mere return, voluntary return as we know it today—or resettlement. But it mentions those only to say this is where refugee status ends. These are cessation clauses. In other words, the 1951 Convention applies only where durable solutions aren't available. In other words, while refugees are still refugees. So we cannot fob that responsibility off on the notion that we're pursuing durable solutions, much as we certainly all are and should be.

Very Little Has Changed

Such a consensus, I think one has to ask, why is it still going on? Why has so little changed? Nobody will defend it but it continues. I think we can go back to that old adage that those of us of a certain age will remember from the 1970s—follow the money. That led to the unraveling of the Watergate scandal but I think it also points to the structural bias of the refugee assistance and protection regime that allows warehousing to continue.

To bring that a little closer to specifics, this is also known in the literature as the relief-to-development gap—the difference between humanitarian assistance on the one hand and development assistance on the other, and the targets of those and the bureaucracies that manage them. In more layperson's terms that you will all recognize, it's like the old adage—give a woman a fish, you've fed her for one day; give her a fishing pole—she can sell the damn thing and buy something that she really needed, but you wouldn't have known if you didn't ask.

Less Humanitarian Assistance, More Development Assistance

Anyway, the point is, people are kept on these humanitarian assistance budgets because all refugee crises start as emergencies. This is where the easiest money to access is. There's less strings attached. You can go in and do the emergency thing that's necessary but then twenty years later, refugees are still on humanitarian budgets. They're still on relief budgets as though it were still an emergency. I defy to say that an emergency can last for generations, but funding-wise, it does. But structurally that creates a whole set of institutions, not only from the tents and huts in the camps, to the aid agencies that provide it, to the UNHCR, to the state governments and the host countries, back to the donor governments that supply the money. The institutions that help integrate people and help people restore livelihoods and be productive—that's a completely different bureaucracy and there's jealously guarded prerogatives and you'll really be viewed as crashing the party to get refugees into development programs.

We're not a development-specialized agency, but I think there's a few things that have consensus in the development world that have emerged over some of the controversies about whether development assistance is really productive or not. It's not settled, but I think there's a few things that have clearly emerged. If you don't have good policy, good governance, you're wasting your money. What the content of that good policy and good governance is involves a lot of things, but it also includes things like allowing people the basic freedom to support themselves and engage in economic activities. The right to work, to practice professions, to run businesses, to own property, freedom of movement—does it sound familiar? These are the rights in the 1951 Convention that the founders said should apply to refugees.

There have been steps made to integrate those principles. I will say that we should approach this from at least two angles.

It's a multifaceted problem. It's been a long time coming here and it'll be a long time gone. Before I get into more depth on the development side, I want to talk about also briefly, although I won't dwell on it, on the humanitarian side.

Assessing Humanitarian Assistance

The humanitarian assistance, which is more geared toward relief, lately has also been going under some self-examination, as well it should be. One of the initiatives has been what's called the Good Humanitarian Donorship Initiative, of which the United States is a part. It's recognized that humanitarian action includes protection and that protection includes human rights standards, specifically including the major human rights agreements, including specifically the 1951 Convention on the status of refugees. So far, so good.

It also includes the principle that restoration of normal livelihoods is an essential goal, objective, of good humanitarian donorship. I say, let's put the two together. If you do that in situations of refugees, of course you have the problem that they are not citizens of the country by definition where they are, so they do not necessarily always have those rights. So that is a mandate that applies to the humanitarian agencies, to move that forward.

Then on the other side, on the development, I want to talk about one particular program that has started in the United States called the Millennium Challenge Account [MCA]. . . .

The Millennium Challenge Account (MCA)

This is an initiative that started with high hopes, and I still have high hopes for it. It was an additional form of assistance and it laid out sixteen criteria under which countries would be judged on eligibility and their proposals would be judged as to whether they advanced them. I won't go into all of them, it's a very complex metric. It takes a while to get a hold of it.

But I'll mention two of the indicators specifically that I think have a great deal of relevance to refugees.

One is called civil liberties, which includes human rights and again, should include all human rights. Another is regulatory quality, which people often don't think of. What's that got to do with refugees? That has to do with starting up businesses and inhibitions to economic activity. Well, if you consider the problems of warehousing, it's not just a matter of—these camps do not have electric fences and guard dogs around them.

What they have is, you have status in that camp, you have no legal status outside. You can eat in the camp, sometimes, but you cannot work outside the camp. You basically have no rights outside. That is the fence. Though in some cases the camps really are more like detention centers. But that is the real gist of it. When we use the term warehousing, it gets a lot of attention. What we do with that attention is draw the attention to the rights of the 1951 Convention.

The Failures of MCA

Where I will say the Millennium Challenge Account has failed is in its metric for judging the civil liberties performance for countries, it takes their score entirely from Freedom House, which is a great organization that's done yeoman's work in human rights in many fields but does not specialize in refugee rights. Its performance in rating refugee rights performance is uneven. I'll just give you some examples. With our 2005 survey, . . . we started analytically breaking down the treatment of refugees in each country along five categories and assigning grades to that performance, measured against the standards of the 1951 Convention. . . . There's a list of countries, major refugee-hosting countries, on which there is no mention or virtually none of the situation of refugee rights. If MCA is going to be using that as their sole metric for civil liberties, then the refugee rights are not going to be included at all.

Development Assistance for Refugees

REFUGEES IN ASYLUM

Refugee Settlements

- Refugees settled in communities and supported by host government/UNHCR and other humanitarian organizations
- Sometimes segregated from local population
- May have access to land for subsistence farming (land not always of good quality)

Local Self-Settlement

- Spontaneous settlements
- Limited access to civil, social and economic rights
- Not fully integrated (legal rights missing)
- Exacerbates migration problems
- Exists in both rural and urban settings

Camps (and other restricted zones)

- Limited self-reliance
- Limited resource generation
- Greater reliance on humanitarian assistance

PREPARING FOR DURABLE SOLUTIONS

Development Assistance for Refugees (DAR)

- Simultaneous improvement of lives and livelihoods (refugees and hosts)
- Focus on medium and long-term development of refugee hosting areas benefiting both host communities and refugees
- Focus on gender/age equality, dignity and improving the quality of life
- Enhancement of productive capacities resulting in self-reliance of refugees
- Empowers refugees to make their own choices for durable solutions
- Broad-based partnership/cooperation with all stakeholders
- Burden-sharing with host community and country
- Promotion of peaceful co-existence

Host Communities

- Poverty alleviation in refugee-hosting areas
- Reduction in disparities between refugees and hosts
- Improved infrastructure and services

Refugees

- Enabling legal environment
- Access to education, skills training
- Income generating opportunities
- Productive and sustainable livelihoods
- Building or strengthening community infrastructures and capacities

DURABLE SOLUTIONS BASED ON SELF-RELIANCE
(Various timeframes needed to be achieved)

Resettlement

- Provides solution for refugees who do not find a durable solution in host country or country of origin
- Requires approval of resettlement request by the resettlement country
- Builds upon refugees capacities attained through DAR

Local Integration

- Requires willingness of host government to integrate refugees
- Allows refugees to integrate within host communities
- Requires mutual acceptance of refugee/host cultures and institutions for co-existence
- Involves a legal, economic, as well as social, cultural and political processes
- Builds upon refugees capacities attained through DAR

Voluntary Repatriation

- Assists in creating an environment which allows refugees to return to their country of origin in safety and dignity
- Promotes durable solutions through repatriation reintegration, rehabilitation and reconstruction (4Rs) activities, poverty reduction and good governance
- Involves key stakeholders in the reintegration process
- Results from returnees capacitated through DAR, thereby facilitating the reintegration process

TAKEN FROM: *Handbook for Planning and Implementing Development Assistance for Refugees (DAR) Programmes*, January 2005.

Bangladesh, one of the most egregious refugee rights violators in the world with the treatment of the Rohingya. China, which refoules North Koreans, sometimes to their deaths—no mention of refugees. Iran, no mention. Kenya, where Kakama camps are, they mention their presence and some criminal activities. I'm sure some refugees do engage in crimes, especially if they're not allowed to work. Malaysia, straight Fs, no mention. The Russian Federation, again, straight Fs in the treatment of refugees and asylum seekers, no mention.

If the MCA is truly going to address refugee rights in their development assistance programs, they're going to have to do better than that. I should say we're not the only game in town on this. PRM [United States Bureau of Population, Refugees, and Migration] has been giving information to the Bureau of Democracy, Human Rights and Labor to include in their country reports. UNHCR has the strengthening protection capacity, which an integral part is doing gaps analyses, which is very much after our own heart in that respect, matching the 1951 Convention standards against the actual treatment. But this is not filtering through.

Another criteria I mentioned, the indicator of economic regulatory quality, which is very central to some of the rights of self-sufficiency for refugees, the sources are almost entirely opaque. They are proprietary sources that the World Bank Institute gathers. In most cases, you can't find them. In the cases that I was able to find them, they generally not only do not mention refugees but many other vulnerable populations [as well]—women, slum-dwellers, other people who ought to count if you're interested in development assistance, if you're interested in actually moving things forward.

The Example of Tanzania

We had high hopes for the MCA, as I recall. I remember when Tanzania was on the threshold, had not really qualified yet but maybe in another year or two, maybe you will. We spoke to the Tanzanian government, met at their embassy, called their finance ministry in Dar es Salaam. They said, you look very interesting. You're from the U.S. Committee for Refugees and Immigrants?

MCA has nothing to do with refugees. Of course, we begged to differ and argued that civil liberties should be interpreted in a certain way and economic regulation and regulatory quality should be interpreted. But another year went by, another set of reports came out absolutely ignoring the treatment of refugees in Tanzania, where there's a four-kilometer rule, where refugees are arrested if they leave beyond 4 kilometers of the camps, and are arrested and sometimes serve up to two years in prison; where they're not even allowed to grow food on the territory of the refugees that have left. Repatriations are in many cases quite questionable as to whether they're voluntary.

I could go on and on, but I won't. Half a million people are being treated like this. I would call this a binding constraint on development, besides being an egregious human rights violation, that ought to be taken into account. Money talks, and it has to be done.

"Thousands of refugees have been pre-vented from resettling in safety in the United States because of these statutory provisions [the material support bar]."

The United States Should Help Refugees Wrongly Accused of Supporting Terrorists

Human Rights First

Human Rights First is a nonprofit, nonpartisan international human rights organization. In the following 2006 report, Abandoning the Persecuted: Victims of Terrorism and Oppression Barred from Asylum, *the authors outline the problems with the material support bar and its application by the U.S. Department of Homeland Security (DHS) and the Department of Justice (DOJ).*

As you read, consider the following questions:

1. What is the material support bar?

2. How has the material support bar hurt many innocent refugees, according to the report?

Eleanor Acer, Anwen Hughes, and Jay Staunton, "Abandoning the Persecuted: Victims of Terrorism and Oppression Barred from Asylum," Human Rights First, 2006. © 2006 Human Rights First. All rights reserved. Reproduced by permission.

3. According to the report, how can the material support problem be rectified?

The United States has a long history of providing safe haven to refugees escaping political oppression and religious persecution in their homelands. But thousands of vulnerable refugees have been prevented from receiving the protection of this country due to overly broad immigration law definitions contained in the USA PATRIOT Act and the REAL ID Act of 2005.

The Material Support Bar

These provisions bar from asylum or resettlement anyone who has provided what the law terms "material support" to "terrorist organizations." The definitions of these terms in the immigration laws, however, and their application by the Department of Homeland Security (DHS) and the Department of Justice (DOJ), are so exceedingly broad that the bar is, tragically, affecting refugees who do not support terrorism at all.

These refugees include: women who were raped and enslaved by armed militias in Liberia; victims of extortion forced to pay armed terrorists in Colombia to protect their lives and their children; and Cubans who supported a group that took up arms against Fidel Castro in the 1960s.

Many of these refugees are actually the *victims* of terrorist violence and extortion in places like Colombia, Nepal and Sri Lanka. Others have provided support to pro-democracy groups with armed wings that have resisted repressive regimes in places like Burma and Cuba, while some supported groups that fought alongside U.S. forces during the war in Vietnam. The U.S. government does not consider these groups to be terrorist organizations in any other context, but because these groups have used arms, they are categorized as terrorist organizations under these immigration law provisions.

The material support bar has crippled the U.S. resettlement program, a unique private-public partnership through

Refugees Need Legislative Support

Congress should clarify immigration law definitions to:

- Provide that refugees who assist groups that would not meet the criteria for designation as foreign terrorist organizations or placement on the Terrorist Exclusion List and that do not present a threat to the security of the United States are not subject to the material support bar. This would ensure the protection of refugees who have supported groups that have resisted the Burmese and other repressive regimes, as well as refugees like the Montagnards, who fought along U.S. troops in Vietnam;

- Specify that only those who are a danger to the national security of the United States, its people or allies are barred; and

- Explicitly recognize that duress is a defense to the material support bar, if the Department of Homeland Security and Department of Justice should fail to recognize the defense implicit in the current statute. . . . This recognition will ensure that qualified refugees who are the victims of coercion can be granted asylum or resettled in the United States.

Human Rights First,
Abandoning the Persecuted: Victims of Terrorism
and Oppression Barred from Asylum, *2006.*

which local communities and church groups across the country assist in welcoming refugees. Thousands of refugees have been prevented from resettling in safety in the United States because of these statutory provisions.

Refugees at Risk

Not only are refugees overseas at risk, but so too are many refugees who have already fled to the United States and applied for asylum in this country. This report addresses the impact of the material support bar on the U.S. asylum system and on refugees who have escaped from persecution and sought asylum in the United States. These refugees have had their asylum requests denied or relegated to a long-term administrative limbo. The time that they have spent in immigration jails—or separated from their families—has been prolonged by months or even years. Among these refugees are:

- A nurse from Colombia who was kidnapped, assaulted and forced to provide medical treatment to terrorists;

- A Christian missionary worker who was beaten and detained by the Burmese military regime and made donations to an armed group that resists the regime and its persecution of Christian minorities;

- A journalist from Nepal who was beaten, threatened and forced to hand over money to Maoists;

- A fisherman from Sri Lanka who was abducted by the Tamil Tigers and forced to pay his own ransom;

- A teacher from Burma who was jailed for two years by the Burmese military after letting three men, who were affiliated with a resistance group, speak in favor of democracy; and

- A student activist and torture survivor who fled Bhutan and was the victim of Maoist extortion while teaching in Nepal. . . .

These refugees and others . . . have had their requests for asylum denied or put on indefinite administrative hold because of the material support bar.

The U.S. Government Is at Fault

While refugees continue to suffer, the various agencies and arms of the U.S. government that are responsible for safeguarding the persecuted have failed to demonstrate the kind of coordination, leadership and commitment that is needed to resolve this problem. . . .

- Some refugees have already been denied asylum by U.S. immigration courts based on these provisions. The denial of these asylum requests places these refugees at grave risk of being returned to danger in violation of the 1951 Refugee Convention and its Protocol, treaties United States has pledged to uphold.

- Hundreds of asylum requests have been placed on indefinite hold at the U.S. asylum office as a result of these provisions and the failure of the Department of Homeland Security to set up an effective process for refugees to seek an exemption. This state of limbo has already lasted several years for some asylum seekers. The delay has left many families separated for years, exposing refugee children to more time in difficult and dangerous circumstances abroad.

- The Department of Homeland Security has detained some refugees affected by this bar in U.S. immigration jails for lengthy periods of time. Several refugees profiled in this report were held for seven months or longer in these jails. One Burmese woman was detained for two years in a Texas immigration jail and a Sri Lankan man has been detained for over a year and a half.

- In individual asylum cases, the Department of Homeland Security and the Department of Justice have taken the position that refugees are barred from asylum even if they were forced to provide the "material support" under duress.

- The Department of Homeland Security, which has lead responsibility for asylum seekers, has resisted necessary and targeted changes to the law, failed to advance administrative policies and procedures to protect some of the refugees affected by this bar, and rejected approaches that would, consistent with the current law, recognize protection for refugees who are victims of terrorism.

Addressing the material support problem will require action by both Congress and the administration. . . . None of these targeted measures would undermine U.S. security. These measures would, however, ensure that this country does not abandon or deport the victims of political oppression and religious persecution who seek its protection.

> "It is the Administration's view that important national security interests and counter-terrorism efforts are not incompatible with our nation's historic role as the world's leader in refugee resettlement."

The United States Should Be Cautious Admitting Refugees Accused of Supporting Terrorists

Paul Rosenzweig

Paul Rosenzweig was the deputy assistant secretary of the Office of Policy Development at the U.S. Department of Homeland Security (DHS), under the President George W. Bush administration. In the following essay, Rosenzweig argues that the material support bar is one of the government's strongest weapons in the fight to keep terrorists and terrorist enablers out of the United States.

Paul Rosenzweig, "The 'Material Support' Bar: Denying Refuge to the Persecuted?" Statement Before the U.S. Senate Judiciary Subcommittee on Human Rights and the Law, *Refugee Council USA*, September 19, 2007.

As you read, consider the following questions:

1. According to new exemptions the author cites, aliens can be admitted even if they gave material support to which two organizations?

2. As of 2007, how many material support exemptions have been granted to applicants for immigration benefits according to Rosenzweig?

3. How many duress-based exemptions have been issued, according to the author?

Under Section 212(a)(3)(B) of the INA [Immigration and Nationality Act], the aliens who provide material support to individuals or organizations that engage in terrorist activity are inadmissible or removable for having engaged in terrorist activity and are ineligible for most immigration benefits. The INA's broad definitions of terrorist activity and the provision of material support to terrorists or terrorist organizations are at the heart of the U.S. government's ability to be proactive in its counter-terrorism efforts. Terrorists need more than ill will to commit terrorist acts; they need funds, equipment, and a variety of other resources to successfully lodge an attack. The Courts and Congress have recognized that "foreign organizations that engage in terrorist activity are so tainted by their criminal conduct that any contribution to such an organization facilitates that conduct." Equipping the U.S. government with the means to take the offensive against those who fuel the maintenance of the terrorist infrastructure, thus, is an essential weapon in the Administration's counter-terrorism arsenal.

The Material Support Bar as a Tool

For DHS [the Department of Homeland Security], with regard to immigration, one of our strongest weapons is the ability to deny benefits or protection to those who have provided material support to terrorists. For example, we successfully used this tool in the case of an alien from Saudi Arabia, who entered the United States as a student. A Joint Terrorism Task Force investigation revealed his connection to the Committee for the Defense of Legitimate Rights (CDLR), an al Qaeda front group. In 2004, U.S. Immigration and Customs Enforcement (ICE)—a component agency of DHS—initiated removal proceedings where an immigration judge found the alien had engaged in terrorist activity through his material support of and his membership to the CDLR. Among other things, he paid for and helped run the CDLR's Web site and solicited money for its operation. The alien was ordered removed and denied any immigration benefits. The alien was successfully removed from the United States in January 2007.

Another example is the case of an alien who was a former board member, fundraiser, and donor to the Benevolence International Foundation (BIF), whose associates in the United States included Aafia Siddiqui (placed on the Federal Bureau of Investigation's Most Wanted Terrorists list after 9/11 [2001 terrorist attacks] for assisting al Qaeda), as well as members of the "Portland 7," a terrorist cell in Portland, Oregon, which conspired to provide material support to al Qaeda and the Taliban during the war against the United States in Afghanistan. The alien applied for adjustment of status to that of a lawful permanent resident, which U.S. Citizenship and Immigration Services (USCIS)—a component agency of DHS—denied: finding the alien had engaged in terrorist activity in the United States by providing material support, including solicitation of funds for BIF, an organization specially designated as a terrorist organization by the U.S. Department of Treasury. The alien was subsequently detained by ICE and placed in removal proceedings. He was removed from the United States in June of 2007.

These cases illustrate this crucial and readily used tool to bar immigration benefits to aliens who provide material support to terrorist organizations.

155

The Material Support Bar Is Used Wisely

While it is vital that DHS is able to use the broad definitions of the INA to prevent aliens who present a genuine threat to the United States or its citizens from entering or staying in the country, it is also our duty to consider providing immigration benefits and protection to deserving aliens who provided material support in sympathetic circumstances, but otherwise are eligible under existing law and who do not pose such a threat. This is especially true in the case of refugees, who may face persecution—sometimes at the hands of the terrorists themselves—if they are not granted the benefits or protection they seek. Because the material support bar casts a broad net, its scope may include those who do not present a risk to U.S. national security and to whom the United States is sympathetic and willing to provide refuge, to the extent allowed by law. It is for this reason that Congress provided in section 212 (d)(3)(B)(i) of the INA that the Secretaries of State and Homeland Security, in consultation with one another and the Attorney General, shall have the discretionary authority not to apply the material support provision in a particular case.

Since the last time I testified, in May of last year [2006], the Administration has worked tirelessly, on an interagency basis, to exercise and implement this authority where doing so is in keeping with the foreign policy and national security interests of the United States. Secretary of State [Condoleezza] Rice exercised this authority three times in 2006 in the refugee program context for Burmese Karen individuals living in various camps in Thailand who provided material support to the Karen National Union (KNU) or Karen National Liberation Army (KNLA) and for Chin refugees from Burma living in Malaysia, India, or Thailand who provided material support to the Chin National Front (CNF) or Chin National Army (CNA). In January 2007, Secretary Rice exercised her authority eight additional times in the refugee program context for refugee resettlement applicants who had provided material support to the following eight organizations: Karen National Union/Karen National Liberation Army (KNU/KNLA), Chin National Front/Chin National Army (CNF/CNA), Chin National League for Democracy (CNLD), Kayan New Land Party (KNLP), Arakan Liberation Party (ALP), Tibetan Mustangs, Cuban Alzados, or Karenni National Progressive Party (KNPP).

In February of this year [2007], Secretary [Michael] Chertoff exercised his authority not to apply the material support inadmissibility provision with respect to certain aliens applying for immigration benefits or protection who had provided material support to these same eight undesignated terrorist organizations for whom Secretary Rice signed exemptions in January. These exercises of authority expanded the scope of the previous exemptions to include asylum seekers and other aliens applying for benefits or protection domestically, as well as refugees applying for protection overseas.

Two New Exemptions

In addition to these eight groups, I am pleased to announce that the Administration has finalized two new exemptions to benefit aliens who have provided material support to certain individuals or groups associated with the Hmong and Montagnard. These exemptions will be issued jointly by the Departments of State and Homeland Security, and are now being prepared for signature by both Secretaries. As both the Hmong and the Montagnards acted as valuable allies to the United States during the Vietnam War, the Administration has long recognized the need to implement exemptions on their behalf.

Also in February of this year [2007], Secretary Chertoff exercised his authority not to apply the material support inadmissibility provision with respect to certain aliens applying for Immigration benefits if the material support was provided under duress to an undesignated terrorist organization or [a] "Tier III" terrorist organization where the totality of the circumstances justify the favorable exercise of discretion. This was the first "duress exemption" either Secretary had exercised. This April [2007], the Secretary of Homeland Security exercised his discretionary authority not to apply the material support bar to individuals who provided the support under duress to certain designated terrorist organizations or "Tier I and II" terrorist organizations if warranted by a totality of the circumstances.

Armed with the above described exemptions, the Administration has turned its attention to implementation of these exercises of authority. DHS has made a great deal of progress in this regard. USCIS has recently completed a tour of all of the asylum offices and two of the service centers handling adjustment of status applications, providing training on material support adjudication procedures.

An Analysis of the Exemptions

So far [in 2007], USCIS has issued over 3,000 exemptions to applicants for immigration benefits who provided material support either to one of the eight named groups or under duress to a terrorist organization. Most of these exemptions have been issued by the Refugee Affairs Division of USCIS. Thus, 2,909 of the exemptions were issued for refugee applicants who provided material support to one of the eight named groups. Most of these exemptions were issued for individuals who provided food and shelter or have assisted in transporting goods for one of the identified groups that opposes the Burmese government. This number includes 295 exemptions issued last fiscal year under the authority granted by Secretary Rice for refugee cases in certain locations. There have also been over 200 exemptions issued to individuals who provided material support to the Cuban Alzados. USCIS has also issued 101 duress-based exemptions. Individuals for whom USCIS issued duress-based exemptions include nationals of Iraq, Liberia, Somalia, and the Democratic Republic of Congo. In addition, Service Center Operations has issued 28 exemptions

What Is Material Support to Terrorism?

A 1996 amendment to the Immigration and Nationality Act (INA) of 1952 extended immigration restrictions against members of terrorist organizations to more indirect affiliates of such groups. It defined, for the first time, the concept of "material support" as the provision of money, goods, personnel, and/or training to terrorist organizations. . . .

The Patriot Act of 2001, the Intelligence Reform and Terrorism Prevention Act of 2004, and the REAL ID Act of 2005 significantly broadened this definition.

In its most up-to-date form, in Title 18 of the United States Code, material support to terrorism is defined as the provision of "any property, tangible or intangible, or service, including currency or monetary instruments or financial securities, financial services, lodging, training, expert advice or assistance, safe houses, false documentation or identification, communications equipment, facilities, weapons, lethal substances, explosives, personnel . . . and transportation, except medicine or religious materials" to terrorist organizations.

This is a nonexclusive list. Department of Homeland Security (DHS) resettlement officers who assess the admissibility of refugee applicants, or immigration judges deciding asylum cases, may declare any other kind of assistance equivalent to material support. For instance, a Burmese pastor's material support consisted of providing a hat and other small articles to a cousin who was a member of the Karen National Union, an antiauthoritarian minority rights group and militia.

Swetha Sridharan, "Material Support to Terrorism—Consequences for Refugees and Asylum Seekers in the United States," Migration Information Source, January 2008. www.migrationinformation.org.

in instances where an applicant sought immigration benefits other than refugee or asylee status, 16 of which were group-based exemptions.

In the case of implementing the Tier I/II duress exemption, the Administration has agreed to a very careful, judicious process to assure that our national security is fully protected even as we fulfill our humanitarian objectives. Prior to beginning processing of cases involving claims of duress by a particular terrorist group, we are obtaining an all-source evaluation concerning that group, its aims and methods, including its use of duress. For instance, one of the goals of the evaluation is to assess whether the Tier I/II terrorist organization may be disposed to use the U.S. Refugee Admissions Program as a conduit to realizing a terrorism-related objective.

A great many of the cases involving the provision of material support under duress to a Tier I terrorist organization that have been adversely affected by the material support bar have involved the provision of material support to the Revolutionary Armed Forces of Colombia (FARC). For that reason, DHS proposed the FARC as the first Tier I group for which an evaluation would be conducted. Based on our review of this evaluation, USCIS has recently begun adjudicating exemptions for the first of these cases.

In addition to the FARC, the Administration has requested evaluations regarding other Tier I/II groups to which a significant number of individuals seeking immigration benefits have stated that they provided material support under duress. As those evaluations are completed and reviewed we will proceed to process additional cases.

Further Amendments Are Needed

While the Administration has made tremendous strides in addressing the unintended consequences of the material support bar through the secretarial exercises of discretionary authority to exempt deserving aliens that have been signed and implemented to date, we remain cognizant of the fact that the authority provided for under INA does not provide the U.S. government with the flexibility to exempt deserving aliens from all of the terrorist provisions for which exemptions would be consistent with U.S. foreign policy and national security objectives. To this end, the Administration submitted proposed legislation to Congress early this year that would amend the INA to allow the U.S. government that needed flexibility. Perhaps most importantly, this legislation would provide the Administration with the authority to exempt certain individuals, such as certain Hmong and Montagnard combatants, who fought valiantly on behalf of the U.S. during the Vietnam War, but who are currently barred and beyond the reach of the secretaries discretionary authority to exempt. In addition, though in some cases the persecutor bar may still apply, the Administration's proposal could allow for the exemption of certain children abducted and forced to undergo military training by armed factions.

It is the Administration's view that important national security interests and counter-terrorism efforts are not incompatible with our nation's historic role as the world's leader in refugee resettlement. While we must keep out terrorists, we can continue to provide safe haven to deserving refugees. Due to national security imperatives, there have been recent changes to the law as well as to the process, and we continue to work on ways to harmonize these two important policy interests. In the last year, we have taken a number of important steps demonstrative of real progress on this front. We have implemented exemptions for aliens who have provided material support to eight Tier III groups and for aliens who have provided material support under duress to Tier I, II, and III groups, and applied these exemptions in both the overseas and domestic contexts. The implementation of these exemptions has yielded impressive results: To date, we have exercised the Secretaries' discretionary authority to exempt over 3,000 deserving aliens from the material support bar, where doing so has been consistent with U.S. national security. As the Department and its interagency partners continue to improve this process, Congress can be assured that the number of deserving aliens who benefit from these exemptions will continue to increase, even as we remain vigilant in executing the mission that Congress has given us to safeguard the security of the American people.

Periodical Bibliography

Doug Bandow   "Feeding a Failing State's Hungry," *San Diego Union-Tribune*, September 15, 2005.

David Case   "Thrown to the Assassins," *Mother Jones*, March–April 2007.

Darryl Fears   "Conservatives Decry Terror Laws' Impact on Refugees," *The Washington Post*, January 8, 2007.

Rebecca Hagelin   "Fleeing to Freedom's Shore," Townhall.com, April 10, 2008.

Parastou Hassouri   "Refugee or Terrorist?" TomPaine.com, December 19, 2006.

Anna Husarka   "When the Law Is the Obstacle for Refugees," *International Herald Tribune*, July 5, 2006.

Eric Johnson-Debaufre "Building a New Sanctuary Movement," *Counterpunch*, May 19, 2006.

Maggie Jones   "The New Yankees," *Mother Jones*, March–April 2004.

Clarence Lusane   "U.S. Must Do More to Help People of Darfur," *The Progressive*, May 3, 2006.

Larry Pratt   "Clueless at Department of Homeland Security," IntellectualConservative.com, March 6, 2006.

Swetha Sridharan   "Material Support to Terrorism—Consequences for Refugees and Asylum Seekers in the United States," Migration Information Source, January 2008. www.migrationinformation.com.

Bethany Stotts   "Refugee or Terrorist?" *Accuracy in Media*, October 11, 2007.

Paul Weyrich   "U.S. Foreign Aid Out of Reason," Townhall.com, November 4, 2008.

What International Policies Can Alleviate the Refugee Problem?

Chapter Preface

The international community, national governments, and non-governmental organizations (NGOs) have developed a number of strategies to address the refugee problem throughout the years. These strategies are known in the refugee assistance community as *durable solutions*. The most popular and effective of these durable solutions include repatriation, resettlement, and integration. As every refugee situation is different, determining the solution that will work for any given crisis requires extensive analysis, widespread cooperation, and concentrated action.

Repatriation is the process of returning refugees to their homeland, hopefully to the very homes they had been forced to leave. Although it seems like the ideal solution, there are often problems with repatriation: homes and surrounding neighborhoods may have been demolished; the political situation may not be settled, which could result in violence or persecution for the repatriated refugees; or the cultural displacement of being back home after being away for some time can hinder a refugee's ability to integrate back into the community.

For many years, *resettlement* was considered to be the ideal solution to the refugee problem. Resettling refugees includes the transfer of refugees from a state in which they have initially sought protection to a third state that has agreed to admit them with permanent-residence status. An example of generally successful resettlement is the Vietnamese boat people, who escaped Vietnam, Cambodia, and Laos in the 1970s and 1980s, spent years in dangerous refugee camps, and were finally resettled in the United States, Australia, and other countries.

Local integration is an option when it is not safe for refugees to return home after a prolonged period in exile, like in a refugee camp. In such cases, a host government may decide to allow refugees to integrate locally and work toward permanent residence and eventual citizenship. It is considered to be a preferable solution to refugee camps, because it encourages economic development and protects refugee rights.

Refugee camps are extremely controversial. There is a growing movement to eliminate *refugee warehousing*, or the herding of refugees into large camps in a host country. Critics of refugee warehousing cite serious health and safety issues, as well as the lack of education and economic opportunities for refugees in such camps. Many feel, however, it is a necessary evil and allows the United Nations High Commissioner for Refugees (UNHCR), national governments, and NGOs to provide a number of important health care and resettlement services to refugees who need them.

Another way to aid refugees is supporting refugee rights. In many cases, establishing a refugee's status is a key step in determining that refugee's future. As such, the refugee status determination process must be completely fair, with consistent rules and a number of safeguards, including a fair appeals process. Without a reasonable system, the rights of individual refugees can be abused.

The following chapter discusses these options in detail, elucidating their strengths as solutions to the refugee problem and their practical limitations in the real world.

> "The agency [United Nations High Commissioner for Refugees] is also guided by the UN [United Nations] declaration on human rights, whose 13th article says that 'everyone has the right to leave any country, including his own, and to return to his country.'"

Safe Repatriation Can Alleviate the Refugee Problem

The Economist

The Economist *is a periodical that focuses on the analysis of world business and current affairs, providing authoritative insight and opinion on international news, world politics, business, finance, science, and technology. In the following viewpoint, the author maintains that although the right for refugees to return to their homeland is paramount, a myriad of factors come into play that may hinder repatriation.*

As you read, consider the following questions:

1. According to the article, how many Iraqis returned to Iraq between June 2007 and March 2008?

2. How many Afghans have returned home since 2002, according to the article?

3. What is the controversy surrounding the return of 4.2 million Palestinian refugees to Israeli land, according to the article?

The scenes look encouraging. Since the beginning of August [2008], hundreds of Iraqi refugees living in Egypt have gone back to their homeland on flights sponsored by the Baghdad authorities. The Iraqi government hails these returns as a sign that things are getting back to normal in a country where more than 2 [million] people have fled abroad, and even more were internally displaced, as a result of the chaos that followed the American-led invasion of 2003.

But away from the fanfare, the feelings of the Iraqis involved in these homecomings are mixed. A few expressed mild optimism that the situation has improved in their home areas. Many more said they were returning because they had little choice: they were unable to work in Egypt and were running out of money.

Nor were they the first of Iraq's refugees to come home. Some 50,000 people re-entered the country in the nine months up to last March [2008] the UN [United Nations] believes. Among these were 365 families who came back from Syria in late 2007, wooed by a resettlement offer of $800 per household. But most of that group later told the UN they could not "go home" in the literal sense; their houses had either been ruined or seized by others.

Ideals vs. Reality

Officials of the UN High Commissioner for Refugees [UN-HCR] also say quietly that the returns from Egypt, insofar as they were prompted by near-destitution, risk violating one of the key principles of refugee law: the idea that people should not be sent back to their home country against their will. But for the UNHCR and other agencies that care for the displaced, this was only the latest of many cases where the high ideals of international law run up against the realities of power politics.

The UNHCR's founding charter is the 1951 Convention on Refugees, which spells out the entitlements of those who flee their country for fear of being killed or persecuted. The agency is also guided by the UN declaration on human rights, whose 13th article says that "everyone has the right to leave any country, including his own, and to return to his own country."

In addition to those principles, many pragmatic considerations guide the actions of governments that take in huge numbers of involuntary migrants. Even if the outside world helps, such arrivals place a huge burden on the receiving country. Refugee camps can be breeding-grounds for extremism; refugees can become political actors in their host country, and their role is often destructive.

All this can be an incentive for receiving countries to "resolve" the fate of refugees on their soil—by sending them home, by resettling them in another country or by finding the right way of integrating them. But that, of course, assumes that the receiving governments want stability. If they want to keep a conflict alive, then keeping an angry population in tents—neither able to go home, nor to settle down anywhere else—can also serve a political purpose.

Afghanistan as a Success Story

Compared with Iraq, the return of refugees to another war-torn land where the West is deeply involved—Afghanistan—has been a relative success story. Over 5 [million] Afghans have returned to their homeland since 2002, mostly from Pakistan and Iran. But 3 [million] Afghans remain in the two neighbouring states; and when António Guterres, the UNHCR chief, met the government of Pakistan (which still hosts 1.8m

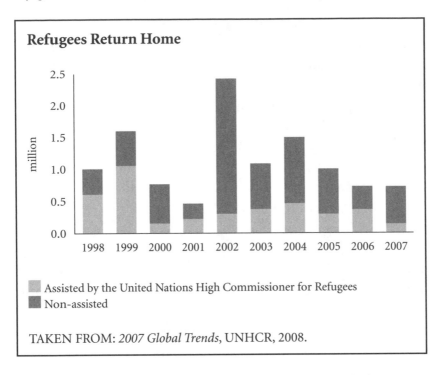

Refugees Return Home

Assisted by the United Nations High Commissioner for Refugees

Non-assisted

TAKEN FROM: *2007 Global Trends*, UNHCR, 2008.

Afghans) last month [August 2008], it was agreed that many refugees are likely to remain on Pakistani soil for years to come.

As the Afghan conflict has shown, the job of the UNHCR does not end when refugees re-enter their homeland. In the early 1990s, the agency's approach to resettling people in their native land was little more than a "cooking-pot and a handshake", says Jeff Crisp, a UNHCR official. Thinking (and the UNHCR's job) broadened under Ruud Lubbers, a former Dutch prime minister, who managed in his time (2001–2005) as head of the agency to breathe new life into some old buzzwords: repatriation, reintegration and rehabilitation. Simply put, people who had fled a country because their village had been flattened would now get more help to go back and take up life where they had left off.

In Iraq and Afghanistan a mass exodus was a by-product of war, and not the conscious or main intention of the country's leaders. Both the outside world and the leaders of Iraq and Afghanistan agree that those countries, in contrast with some other conflict zones, should continue to exist within their present borders, and that a mixture of sects and ethnicities should live in them.

The Cases of Bosnia and Kosovo

Things are harder when war is triggered by an openly nationalistic project that seeks to redraw borders and change demographic balances; the most obvious, but not the sole, case of this in recent European history was the effort by [former president] Slobodan Milosevic to forge a greater Serbia.

With more consistency than has been applied in other places, the settlements imposed on Balkan war zones reflected the very opposite idea: the idea that "ethnic cleansing will not stand", so that anybody who was forced to abandon home and property must be allowed, and helped, to go back. That looked optimistic at the time of the Dayton accords, which settled the Bosnian war in 1995. Nearly half the country's pre-war population had been uprooted; about 1m [million] had taken refuge abroad, and as many again were internally displaced. A decade later, statistics at least suggested a great achievement. Just over 1m [million] Bosnians had reclaimed their homes, and of these nearly half were so-called minority returns, going back to places where a rival group was dominant.

On closer inspection, however, the Bosnian record isn't quite so spectacular. A report published last month [August 2008] noted that in many cases, claimed "returns" meant simply that a displaced proprietor reasserted his title and then rented out or sold his old home. And the dream of remaking mixed communities was only a partial success, says Andy Bearpark, a Briton who oversaw the Bosnian effort.

In Kosovo, too, much energy was devoted to helping the return of people displaced by war, even if they had to take the risk of coexisting with old foes. That effort got under way in

August 2001, when 54 Serbs were driven at night, under heavy international guard, to an area in western Kosovo where they had once lived. But the security surrounding that operation underlined the hard truth that in Kosovo's embittered atmosphere, recreating an ethnic mix depends on a huge policing operation; once the field is left to local players, the cycle of cleansing may restart. In all, only 18,000 "minority returns" (out of a possible total of over 100,000) are claimed for Kosovo, and many did not stay long.

As part of the price of Western recognition for their independence, Kosovo's leaders agreed that their land should have room for non-Albanian minorities. But in reality nationalist Kosovars—like every other ethnic faction in the region—hardly hide their feeling that the fewer minorities they have to live with, the better.

A Difficult Issue

That leads on to the hardest question of all for anyone concerned with refugees: is the right of return a principle on which no negotiation is possible, or is it simply one of several considerations, on which there can be political trade-offs? To put it another way, can governments limit a right that is ascribed unconditionally to individuals—the right of displaced people to decide whether or not to return home?

Israeli officials cite the more pragmatic view to make a case against any automatic right of return for the 4.2m [million] Palestinians—refugees from the 1948 war, and their descendants—who may in theory reclaim homes or land on the territory of Israel. UN resolution 194, voted by the General Assembly in 1948, is often quoted in support of the Palestinian right of return: it says that "refugees wishing to return to their homes and live at peace with their neighbours should be permitted to do so at the earliest practicable date." Israelis insist that, far from proclaiming a non-negotiable principle, this language subordinates return to other considerations, such as feasibility and the intentions of the refugees.

In any case, the "right of return" has snarled all efforts to seal a final Israeli-Palestinian peace. On the Israeli side, it is claimed that anybody who asserts this right is demanding the end of the Jewish state and cannot really want peace. Ehud Olmert, the outgoing prime minister, says Israel need take no refugees back because it was not responsible for the 1948 war; Palestinians retort that many expulsions took place before that war. Conscious that a "right of return" can neither be accepted by Israelis nor ignored by Palestinians, the [President George W.] Bush administration has suggested that the right be exercised in a modified form: Palestinians could return to a new Palestinian state emerging out of a two-state solution, but not to Israel.

If a desire for peace really existed on all sides, that approach might possibly work—but only if it were accepted that the right of return is something to be negotiated, not simply asserted.

> "The ... functions of resettlement ... would indicate that it is most effective when applied as part of a comprehensive approach to international protection."

Resettlement Can Help Solve the Refugee Problem

United Nations High Commissioner for Refugees

The United Nations High Commissioner for Refugees (UNHCR) is a United Nations agency responsible for the protection and support of refugees in the international community. In the following viewpoint, the UNHCR describes the basic functions of resettlement and discusses it as a durable solution to the refugee problem.

As you read, consider the following questions:

1. According to the viewpoint, how many of the Vietnamese "boat people" were resettled as a result of the 1989 Comprehensive Plan of Action for Indochina?

2. What were the new resettlement countries to emerge by 2001, according to UNCHR?

3. What are the three functions of resettlement that the
   UNHCR lists?

Resettlement may be defined as the transfer of refugees from a state in which they have initially sought protection to a third state that has agreed to admit them with permanent-residence status. Until the mid-1980s, resettlement was generally seen by states as the preferred durable solution. In the aftermath of the Second World War it was the primary means by which the International Refugee Organization and, later, UNHCR [United Nations High Commissioner for Refugees] provided solutions for the displaced. It was used to resettle nearly 200,000 refugees following the 1956 Hungarian revolution, more than 40,000 people expelled from Uganda by Idi Amin in 1972, and 5,000 Latin American refugees facing *refoulement* from Augusto Pinochet's Chile in 1973. Perhaps most notably, resettlement was used to address the problem of the Vietnamese 'boat people', of whom nearly 2 million were resettled as a result of the 1989 Comprehensive Plan of Action (CPA) for Indochina. Yet despite the example of the CPA, resettlement elsewhere was limited to the often-unfilled quotas of a handful of traditional resettlement states. By the 1990s, repatriation had taken centre stage.

However, since the end of the CPA in 1995 there has been ongoing reflection and reassessment of the role of resettlement. Following UNHCR's 1994 Evaluation Report on Resettlement Activities, the Working Group on Resettlement was formed that same year, and shortly afterwards UNHCR's Annual Tripartite Consultations (ATC) on resettlement began. These consultations have become a forum in which resettlement countries, NGOs [non-governmental organizations] and UNHCR share information and develop joint strategies to address resettlement needs. Alongside the ATC, the Working Group began to reassess the role of resettlement and promote the emergence of new resettlement countries and the expansion of quotas. As a result, the global resettlement quota grew

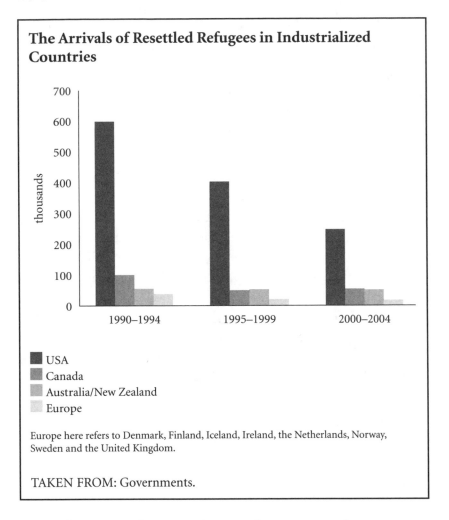

The Arrivals of Resettled Refugees in Industrialized Countries

USA
Canada
Australia/New Zealand
Europe

Europe here refers to Denmark, Finland, Iceland, Ireland, the Netherlands, Norway, Sweden and the United Kingdom.

TAKEN FROM: Governments.

to nearly 100,000 by 2001. Among the new resettlement countries to emerge are Argentina, Benin, Brazil, Burkina Faso, Chile, Iceland, Ireland, Spain and the United Kingdom.

Policy and practice in relation to resettlement have therefore undergone significant changes in recent years. The strategic use of resettlement and new operational methods such as group identification and processing are enhancing resettlement's traditional function of protection. These innovations have been consolidated within the Multilateral Framework of Understandings on Resettlement, agreed in June 2004.

The Functions of Resettlement

Resettlement formed a central component of the Global Consultations. In the context of a comprehensive strategy to enhance international protection, discussions on resettlement highlighted that it has three central functions. Its first—and traditional—role is as a tool of international protection for individual refugees. Second, it may serve as a durable solution. This reflects acknowledgement that resettlement can be used alongside other durable solutions as part of a comprehensive strategy to overcome protracted refugee situations. Finally, resettlement may be an expression of international solidarity. Resettlement by third states represents a commitment to a more equitable sharing of responsibility for protection with the developing countries that host the majority of the world's refugees.

However, questions remain about resettlement and its relationship to the other durable solutions. On the one hand, it may be seen as a symbol of extra-regional states' willingness to share responsibility; on the other, it may represent a disincentive to repatriation by encouraging some refugees to remain in the host state hoping to be resettled.

The Strategic Use of Resettlement

The three complementary functions of resettlement—as a protection tool, a durable solution and an expression of international burden-sharing—would indicate that it is most effective when applied as part of a comprehensive approach to international protection. Indeed, it was in the broader multilateral context of the Convention Plus initiative that the Core Group on Resettlement was created. The group drafted the Multilateral Framework of Understandings on Resettlement, building on the prior initiatives of the Working Group on Resettlement and the Global Consultations on International Protection.

In recent years more emphasis has been placed on the strategic use of resettlement. This conceives of 'the planned use of resettlement that maximizes the benefit of resettlement, either directly or indirectly, other than to those being resettled. Those benefits accrue to other refugees, the host States, other States, and the international protection regime in general'. Such strategic use of resettlement acknowledges that it is likely to be most effective when applied alongside the other durable solutions in situation-specific plans of action. For example, this might apply when a small group represents a stumbling block in the way of peace negotiations or a wider repatriation agreement. Here resettlement, even of small groups, may serve as a catalyst in leveraging other solutions.

The Group Methodology

Aside from presenting many of the general principles underlying resettlement, the Multilateral Framework also elaborated the role of the Group Methodology, developed in 2003 to enhance the use of resettlement. Group resettlement covers not only specific vulnerable individuals, but also groups that are in protracted refugee situations. By focusing on a section of the refugee population on the basis of identity characteristics such as clan, ethnicity, age or gender, for example, it may enhance the search for durable solutions. It would benefit not only the group in question, but also those not resettled by removing a vulnerable section of the population from a given situation. Group resettlement is designed to supplement traditional resettlement activities. It does not replace the responsibility of UNHCR to identify and process individual resettlement cases based on established criteria.

Resettlement countries and other partners have welcomed the Group Methodology and participated in missions to locations where refugee populations have been identified for possible resettlement. Examples of refugee groups processed for resettlement in 2003–04 include:

- Liberians in Côte d'Ivoire and Sierra Leone resettled in the United States;

- Liberians in Guinea resettled in Australia and the United States;

- Somalis in Kenya resettled in Australia, Canada and the United States; and

- Ethiopians in Yemen resettled in the United States.

> *"Considering the protracted nature of most refugee-producing crises and the unsuitability of refugee camps as the primary means for addressing these situations, it is imperative that alternative strategies are tested and, where they are found to be potentially viable and preferable, implemented."*

Integration Can Alleviate the Refugee Problem

Sarah J. Feldman

Sarah J. Feldman works with immigrants and refugees on behalf of Migration and Refugee Services at the U.S. Conference of Catholic Bishops. In the following viewpoint, she views integration into host communities as a viable option for refugees warehoused in refugee camps for long periods of time.

As you read, consider the following questions:

1. How many millions of refugees have been living in refugee camps for five years or more, according to the author?

Sarah J. Feldman, "Development Assisted Integration: A Viable Alternative," *PRAXIS, The Fletcher Journal of Human Security*, 2007. © 2007 PRAXIS, The Fletcher School, Tufts University. Reproduced by permission.

2. How many refugees does the author say have been in camps for more than ten years?

3. What are the three durable solutions to the refugee problem as listed by the United Nations High Commissioner for Refugees (UNHCR)?

Since the inception of the refugee protection regime in 1951, refugee camps have been its central organizing concept. In the camp-based model, refugee-producing crises are assumed to be temporary emergencies. In reality, most refugee situations last much longer: 7.89 million of the world's 12 million refugees and asylum seekers have been in camps for five years or more. . . . Development assisted integration (DAI) is an alternative paradigm, which has had some success getting refugees out of camps and moving toward self-sufficiency and greater enjoyment of their rights in protracted crises. However, there remains a lack of research on the viability of such an approach, as well as a number of challenges to implementation. . . .

Fixing the Problem of Refugee Camps

Refugee-producing crises are mostly assumed to be temporary emergencies in which the camp will serve as an impermanent settlement where refugees' basic needs are met until they can return home, likely within a few months. In reality however, most refugee situations last much longer than this, and 7.13 million [refugees] have been [in camps] for 10 or more years. These "warehoused" populations range from Congolese refugees living in camps for seven years to Palestinians in Gaza, Lebanon, and the West Bank who have been living as refugees for 57 years. Over two million Afghans have been in Iranian and Pakistani camps for 26 years. While camps are certainly necessary in the emergency phase of a refugee crisis, as well as in a limited capacity afterwards, reliance on a camp-centric policy in protracted refugee situations is an inefficient use of resources, which causes tension between refugee and local populations, keeps refugees dependent on aid, can lead to health and security crises, and prevents refugees from reentering society and pursuing livelihoods.

Considering the protracted nature of most refugee-producing crises and the unsuitability of refugee camps as the primary means for addressing these situations, it is imperative that alternative strategies are tested and, where they are found to be potentially viable and preferable, implemented. One alternative approach to camps, which has had some measure of success, is that which I will call Development Assisted Integration (DAI). Local integration entails the voluntary settlement of refugees in the communities of the host country. In this model, refugees leave camps either by becoming economically self-sufficient or by choosing to remain after a camp closes and receiving assistance from the United Nations High Commissioner for Refugees (UNHCR). DAI refers to the coordination of refugee assistance with local economic development so that those communities that host refugees can receive additional funding for enabling refugees to settle amongst locals by strengthening the services and livelihood opportunities available to both populations. However, there remains a lack of research on the viability of these kinds of alternatives, the specific challenges to implementing them, and the set of obstacles that stand in the way of selling these alternative policies to UNHCR, host governments, local populations, donors, and refugees. . . .

The Official Status of Refugees

According to the 1951 Convention relating to the Status of Refugees, a refugee is an individual with a well-founded fear of persecution on the grounds of race, religion, nationality, membership in a social or political group; is outside the country of his or her origin; and, due to this fear, is unable or unwilling to afford the protection of that country. Before pro-

Refugee Integration and Citizenship

The limited data on naturalization of refugees available to UNHCR [United Nations High Commissioner for Refugees] show that during the past decade, more than 1 million refugees were granted citizenship by their asylum country. The United States of America alone accounted for more than half of them, even though their 2007 numbers are not yet available. Azerbaijan and Armenia also granted citizenship to a significant number of refugees during the same period (188,400 and 65,000 respectively). UNHCR was informed of refugees being granted citizenship in Belgium (12,000), the United Republic of Tanzania (730), Armenia (700), Finland (570), and Ireland (370).

United Nations High Commissioner for Refugees, 2007
Global Trends: Refugees, Asylum-Seekers, Returnees,
Internally Displaced and Stateless Persons, 2008.

ceeding, it will be helpful to distinguish the various groups of displaced persons, which are sometimes referred to as refugees. People who cross a border in flight are officially called asylum seekers, while refugees have been conferred that status by the state based on the definition of a refugee in the 1951 Convention. Because this distinction guarantees a refugee a number of sought after rights, protections, and benefits, host states are reluctant to confer this status. The vast majority of "refugees" in Africa are actually asylum seekers, as they do not have official refugee status, but as is common practice, I will refer to both asylum seekers and those who have been conferred refugee status as refugees.

By the end of 2005 there were 20.8 million people of concern to UNHCR, including refugees, asylum seekers, internally displaced persons, and stateless persons. Refugees and asylum seekers made up 58 percent of this total in 2005, numbering approximately 12 million. While the number of refugees in the world grew gradually during the 1970s and dramatically during the 1980s, today that number is decreasing slightly. Refugee and asylum seeker totals in recent years have ranged from 11.5 million in 2004 to 13.5 million in 1998 to 14.9 million in 2001.

Three Durable Solutions

UNHCR utilizes and promotes three durable solutions to refugee problems: repatriation, resettlement, and local integration. Repatriation, which is assisting refugees in voluntarily returning home once an area has again become safe, is the preferred solution. Resettlement is a viable option for a very small number of the world's refugees (84,809 out of 11.5 million total refugees in 2005), and is intended to be reserved for those who are not secure in the country of first asylum and who would not be safe to return home even if hostilities there ceased. As set out in international refugee conventions, local integration as a durable solution refers to the granting of full and permanent asylum, membership, and residency status by the host government. Refugees with full residency status enjoy the range of rights established in the 1951 Convention, including the right to work, of access to education and housing, to own property, and to practice one's own religion. However, this status is granted to so few refugees in developing countries that . . . the term local integration will connote the self-settlement or planned settlement of refugees amongst a local population, regardless of their official status.

> *"Refugees should enjoy the same human rights as any other people. However, refugees have traditionally been relegated to the category of 'humanitarian' problems, the human rights dimension of their plight being generally ignored."*

Supporting Refugee Rights Can Help the Refugee Problem

Barbara Harrell-Bond and Mike Kagan

Barbara Harrell-Bond is Distinguished Visiting Professor for the Forced Migration and Refugee Studies Programme at American University in Cairo, Egypt. Mike Kagan is a refugee law specialist. In the following viewpoint, the authors assess current refugee status determination (RSD) procedures, maintaining that reforms are needed that recognize and support refugee rights.

As you read, consider the following questions:

1. What is the importance of being officially classified as a refugee, according to the authors?

Barbara Harrell-Bond and Mike Kagan, "Protecting the Right of Refugees in Africa," *Pambazuka News*, November 11, 2004. Reproduced by permission.

2. How many countries have handed over their refugee status determination (RSD) duties to the United Nations High Commissioner for Refugees (UNHCR)?

3. According to independent studies, what is wrong with UNHCR's RSD procedures?

The lack of attention to the ways in which refugees' rights are violated in host countries is astonishing if one considers that the protection of the rights of all people has been on the United Nations (UN) agenda since the adoption of the Universal Declaration of Human Rights, and that refugees have formed an important part of the UN's work since the Second World War. Refugees should enjoy the same human rights as any other people. However, refugees have traditionally been relegated to the category of 'humanitarian' problems, the human rights dimension of their plight being generally ignored.

In practice, to enjoy the most basic human security, it is not enough today for an asylum-seeker to be a human being, S/he must obtain the formal label "refugee" to enjoy even legal recognition as a person in most countries. Without this label, a person will find themselves in fear of the state rather than protected by a government. Living without documents, without UNHCR [UN High Commissioner for Refugees] or government protection, places refugees at imminent risk of detention and refoulement [return to a place where they would face persecution]. It leaves them vulnerable to exploitations large and small by their neighbors, landlords, and employers.

After 'getting in' to a country, the determination of refugee status is the most critical challenge that people in danger face when they seek protection. There is a growing tendency in Africa to put individual refugees through the process of individual status determination, rather than group-based recognition.

Refugee Status Determination Is the First Step

The UN High Commissioner for Refugees (UNHCR) has said that 'the importance of these procedures cannot be overemphasized ... a wrong decision might cost the person's life or liberty'. For UNHCR, fair refugee status determination (RSD) procedures are 'essential' for full application of the 1951 Convention. The General Assembly has repeatedly referred to the need to establish 'fair and efficient procedures' in the asylum process.

Being granted status is also the first step towards refugees taking an active part in governing their own lives and future. Determining their status is the responsibility of the state where they seek asylum. However, in over 60 countries—mainly in Africa, the Middle East and Asia—the local office of the UN-HCR handles RSD, making it nearly the largest RSD decision-maker in the world. The fact that so many states have handed this responsibility over to UNHCR (more than half have ratified the 1951 Convention) is indicative of how little some governments have done to implement the Convention, shifting responsibility instead to the UN.

When UNHCR fills the gap, refugees and governments should be able to rely on UNHCR to perform such an essential role in keeping with the highest standards. When human rights groups raise alarm about a government's refugee policies, they usually call for UNHCR to have more access. UN-HCR has given progressive, legally sound advice to governments about RSD. UNHCR is responsible for supervising refugee law, and refugees ought to be able to trust that in UNHCR's hands their rights will be respected. Yet, on RSD, UNHCR is saying one thing to governments, and doing something much worse.

RSD Procedures Are Flawed

UNHCR's RSD procedures have been assessed independently by lawyers, scholars, and human rights organizations in the

Middle East, Southeast Asia and East Africa. Their conclusions are the same: UNHCR's RSD procedures lack the most basic safeguards of fairness, resulting in a high chance of mistakes in a field where there simply is no margin for error. There is an unacceptable risk that people in grave danger will be refused protection when they apply to UNHCR offices. Furthermore, by not following its own advice about RSD procedures, UNHCR sets a bad example for states. The system is broken and needs to be fixed.

What exactly is wrong with UNHCR's Refugee Status Determination?

The essential problem with UNHCR conducting refugee status determination is that by assuming the role of decision-maker, it compromises its role as protector of refugees with that of being 'judge and jury' of their claims. These are contradictory roles and wherever UNHCR places itself in this situation, it loses the trust of refugees. Secondly, its RSD practices lack procedural safeguards and fairness. They are hence high risk for error, and can put people in danger of refoulement in fact if not refoulement in form.

Despite being absent from the text of the refugee conventions, UNHCR has issued fairly comprehensive specific procedural requirements for fair RSD. The earliest attempt conclusions of the Executive Committee of the UNHCR (EXCOM) . . . and the *Handbook on Procedures and Criteria for Determining Refugee Status* (1992), set out basic procedural requirements. State practice has also over the years fleshed out standards of procedural fairness that apply to refugee status determination, both through case-law and through statutes or administrative regulations. UNHCR has now issued more comprehensive advice to states about standards necessary for a fair and effective RSD procedure. In May 2001, as part of its Global Consultations on International Protection, UNHCR issued its most comprehensive guidance, on RSD procedures to date, a background paper called "Fair and Efficient Asylum

Procedures." UNHCR added to this guidance in February 2003 with comments submitted to the Council of Europe.

The standards UNHCR has set out are admirable. But, for whatever reason, UNHCR itself has not seen fit to follow them.

The UNHCR Does Not Follow Its Rules

We detail a number of specific problems:

Secret evidence. Withholding evidence considered in an applicant's case—which the applicant involved cannot see or dispute—is a familiar (and very worrisome) part of military and state security trials, but with rare exception it should not be part of RSD. UNHCR told the Council of Europe, "UN-HCR [. . .] recommends that information and its sources may be withheld only under clearly defined conditions where disclosure of sources would seriously jeopardize national security or the security of the organizations or persons providing information."

But in its own RSD procedures, UNHCR offices withhold nearly all evidence from asylum-seekers, in accordance with a confidential August 2001 memorandum from the Department of International Protection. Evidence routinely withheld from asylum-seekers includes reports from mental health assessments and medical examinations, transcripts of their own interviews, statements by other witnesses, and country of origin information.

Reasons for rejection. UNHCR has advised governments that refused asylum-seekers "should receive a written decision . . . [and] the decision should be a reasoned one." But when UNHCR refuses a refugee claim, its offices generally refuse to provide detailed written reasons that could be used in preparing an appeal. In some offices, the person receives a letter with just one or two sentences explaining the rejection. In other offices, rejected applicants get only a three-letter code, such as "LOC" (lack of credibility). Some UNHCR offices give no explanation at all. At the same time, UNHCR offices write, and keep on file, detailed assessments of each case.

Independent appeals. Since 1980, UNHCR has called on governments to provide rejected asylum-seekers with access to an Independent appeal. In 2001, UNHCR said that this appeal must be to "an authority different from and independent of that making the initial decision," But in most UNHCR offices, the only appeal is to a different staff member in the same office, usually a colleague of the person who made the original rejection, working under the same supervisors.

Refugees Should Have Legal Support

Right to counsel. UNHCR has advised governments that "at all stages of the procedure, including at the admissibility stage, asylum-seekers should receive guidance and advice on the procedure and have access to legal counsel."

In a few UNHCR offices, the principle of legal representation is accepted. But other offices resist the right to counsel. Some UNHCR offices refuse to accept submissions by lawyers. Others refuse to speak with lawyers about their clients' cases. Still others have questioned asylum-seekers about why they chose to seek legal assistance. In one UNHCR office in the Middle East, a protection officer recently insisted that an indigent refugee pay a significant fee to a notary in order to be represented by a lawyer in a hearing over whether UNHCR would withdraw his refugee status.

Behind these failures are fundamental questions of transparency and accountability. By withholding evidence and the reasons for rejection, UNHCR shields its actions from scrutiny. But this tendency toward secrecy goes beyond individual cases. UNHCR's RSD operating procedures are generally not released to the public. The Department of International Protection (DIP) memorandum instructing UNHCR offices to withhold evidence from asylum-seekers was never circulated to the public for comment, and to this day it is officially internal.

UNHCR has indicated that it is drafting a new handbook governing its RSD activities, but it has not yet asked for public comment. It is worrisome to think that procedural standards are being re-debated within UNHCR simply because this time UNHCR offices are meant to apply them. There is no plausible reason why the legal standards of UNHCR's RSD procedures should differ from the high standard that it recommends to governments. When UNHCR tells the public that certain standards are essential for refugee protection, these standards should automatically be implemented in UNHCR's own offices.

Finding Alternatives to RSD

Although reforming RSD procedures themselves is urgent, it is also important to reduce their importance. Individual RSD is, as a rule, intensive, burdensome on all involved, high stakes, and high risk for error. The more UNHCR and governments can find other ways to recognize refugee status, the better.

In cases of mass movements where it is impracticable to conduct individual status determination of refugees seeking asylum, governments may grant prima facie [on first appearance] recognition to the group on the basis of nationality. Prima facie recognition may be granted either under the 1951 Convention or the Organisation of African Unity (now African Union) Convention (OAU).

This makes sense; it reflects the practice in post-World War II Europe when all refugees were recognized on the grounds of nationality. When [Fridtjof] Nansen, appointed by the League of Nations, was first named Commissioner for Russian Refugees [in 1921], all Russian refugees in Europe after the revolution were entitled to recognition. Similarly, everyone knows there is war in southern and western Sudan; people fleeing that war should simply have to 'prove' their nationality.

Decisions to grant prima facie recognition to particular nationalities should be 'gazetted', i.e. as legal decisions they must be published officially. This is only the first step; every adult refugee must be issued with an identity card. The Conclusion of the Executive Committee of UNHCR (EXCOM), in 1993, also reiterated the necessity of the issuing of personal documentation as a device to promote the protection of the personal security of refugees.

Nansen went much further. Realizing that movement was necessary to find solutions to their plight, the Nansen Passport was introduced, allowing refugees to move to another country where they could find, for example, employment or education or re-join relatives. The Nansen passport thus served refugees as a passport, allowing them to travel between states. It was the forerunner of today's Convention Travel Document (CTD). Article 28 of the 1951 UN Convention provides that 'Contracting States' shall issue travel documents, that is, CTDs to refugees lawfully in their territories for the purpose of travel outside their territories. (There are only two reasons for which Contracting State can deny refugees this right: compelling reasons of national security or public order.)

In Africa, where most refugees are sent to camps or settlements, the only identification the vast majority receive is a family ration card, which usually includes only an indication of the size of the family with marks to punch when rations are received or non-food items are distributed, not their name.

What is being done?

Evaluating RSD Procedures

At the International Council of Voluntary Agencies (ICVA) Pre-Executive Committee October 2004 meetings, four lawyers from Africa and the Middle East successfully lobbied for ICVA to call for an independent evaluation of UNHCR RSD. The following are excerpts from final NGO [non-governmental organization] Statement to UNHCR's Executive Committee on Evaluation and Inspection Activities:

> We would suggest that such an independent global evaluation be carried out by a team that includes international human rights lawyers, international and national NGOs working on refugee issues, academics, and legal aid practitioners. The issues that should be examined in the evaluation include an inventory of the RSD procedures that are applied in each UNHCR field office, with an examination of the possible solutions to the political, financial, and human resource constraints that contribute to RSD procedures that do not fulfill practices advocated by UNHCR. The evaluation should recommend rights-based RSD procedures to be followed consistently by all field protection officers with a mechanism to ensure their implementation.

And from the Statement on Protection:

> Further, while recognising the important role played by UNHCR in asylum determination procedures in many countries worldwide, NGOs have concerns that some of UNHCR's refugee status determination (RSD) practices in some countries in Africa, the Middle East, and Asia do not always meet the standards of fairness to which UNHCR urges states to adhere. . . . UNHCR should not see its role in RSD as a substitute for government-run procedures. UNHCR should make it a priority that governments take over these activities and build their capacity to do so. We call on UNHCR to initiate public consultations on the new draft refugee status determination procedures.

What Individuals Can Do

It will be important to follow this initiative carefully over the next year and at the 2005 ICVA Pre-Excom meetings to ensure the issue is actively followed up. What can you do?

The Human Rights of Refugees

The human right to seek and enjoy asylum from persecution.

The human right not to be forcibly returned to the country he or she is fleeing. . . .

The human right to freedom of movement, freedom to choose his or her residence, freedom to leave any country. . . .

The human right to freedom from discrimination based on race, colour, gender, language, religion, nationality, ethnicity, or any other status.

The human right to equal protection of the law, equal access to the courts, and freedom from arbitrary or prolonged detention.

The human right to a nationality.

The human right to life.

The human right to protection from torture. . . .

The human right to freedom from genocide. . . .

The human right to an adequate standard of living, including adequate food, shelter and clothing.

The human right to work. . . .

The human right to the highest possible standard of health and to access to health care.

The human right to live in a healthy and safe environment.

The human right to education.

The human right to participation in decision-making which affects a refugee's life, family, and community.

The human right to sustainable development.

The human right to peace.

People's Movement for Rights Education,
"Human Rights and Refugees," 2009. www.pdhre.org.

The first step to change the situation for refugees is to inform yourself. While presuming that readers of *Pambazuka News*, are committed to human rights, too few human rights organisations consider refugee rights as part of their mandate. In your country, as in so many, refugees are probably segregated in camps and those who manage to live elsewhere are usually trying to remain invisible to authorities for the reasons of lack of proper papers and the right to live outside of camps. Join the US Committee for Refugees [and Immigrants (USCRI)] anti-warehousing campaign and begin to study and expose the way refugee rights are being violated in your country. Lobby for their minimal right to freedom of movement.

For those who think of refugees as 'just another problem among so many', remember that getting it right for refugees may be the best way to get rights for all! Is not the extent to which refugee rights are upheld, a barometer for the extent that human rights are generally respected in any society? Human rights are indivisible, interrelated and inter-related; focusing on the violations of the rights of refugees (who represent the most marginalized and unprotected population) is perhaps the most effective 'entry' point for improving the observance of human rights for all members of any society. Any investment in promoting the rights of refugees is an investment in a more just society.

Legal Aid Clinics for Refugees

Find out if there are any legal aid clinics in your country who would be in a position to represent refugee clients whatever their problems might be and encourage them to consider getting the necessary training to expand their clients to include refugees. The Forced Migration and Refugee Studies Programme at the American University in Cairo and AMERA Egypt, a refugee legal aid clinic both provide training opportunities. Oxfam, through Reach Out also offers a Refugee Protection Training Project for all NGOs. Where legal aid clinics for refugees exist, support their work and see how you might get involved.

Clinics providing legal aid for refugees have been established in a few countries in the 'south', in Africa, in 1999, the Refugee Law Project in Kampala; the Kenyan Refugee Consortium, Nairobi; AMERA-Egypt in Cairo. Others are the Frontiers Centre in Lebanon and the Istanbul Refugee Legal Aid Project in Turkey.

In the end, two points are absolutely essential. First, don't rely blindly on the UN. A strong UN is essential for a just and peaceful world, but that does not mean that UN agencies can be trusted anymore than governments. They must be transparent, they must be accountable, and we must watch to make sure they practice what they preach.

Second, this entire discussion has been devoted to how we determine whether a person is a "refugee" under the law. But we ought to remember: We don't need UNHCR or a complicated procedure to recognize another person as a human being. And that ought to be enough to give refugees the most essential human rights.

| *"Because of security concerns, refugee camps are frequently the only remedy."*

Refugee Camps Are a Necessary Evil

Voice of America

The Voice of America (VOA) is a multimedia international broadcasting service that broadcasts news, information, educational, and cultural programming, and is funded by the U.S. government. In the following viewpoint, the VOA reports that although many officials perceive refugee camps to be detrimental to individuals, there are others who argue that camps are a necessary evil because they keep refugees safer than they would be on their own.

As you read, consider the following questions:

1. How many refugees is the United Nations High Commissioner for Refugees (UNHCR) caring for in how many countries, according to the Voice of America?

2. According to UNHCR, how many refugees has it helped in the past 50 years?

3. How do donors influence UNHCR's actions, according to the article?

Voice of America, "Refugee Camps: Good for Africa or a Necessary Evil?" January 9, 2003. Reproduced by permission.

Where there is conflict, there are refugees. Thousands—and in some cases—millions of people looking for safe haven. Many, if not most, end up in refugee camps—sometimes for months, sometimes for many years. But are the camps good for refugees and good for Africa? Or are they, as some call them, a necessary evil?

The UN [United Nations] refugee agency—the UN High Commissioner for Refugees [UNHCR]—currently cares for nearly 20 million people in 120 countries. Most refugees are in Asia, nearly 9 million. Europe ranks second at almost 5 million, while Africa has more than 4 million refugees.

UNHCR's Involvement Is in Question

The UNHCR's mandate is "to lead and coordinate international action to protect refugees and resolve refugee problems worldwide." It says in the last 50 years, it has helped about 50 million people.

However, the acting director of Forced Migration and Refugee Studies at American University in Cairo questions the UNHCR's methods. Barbara Harrell-Bond says camps are bad not only for refugees, but for the host countries as well.

She says, "The main concern, of course, is that people in most situations lack freedom of movement, which is a fundamental human right upon which all other rights are conditional or contingent. The second issue is the fact that UNHCR spends enormous amounts of money establishing refugee camps and setting up parallel programs of health, education and so on rather than using these resources to strengthen local institutions so they can absorb the refugees."

She says refugee camps "are often prison-like places that no one wants to live in and those who can, escape."

She says, "Refugees are human beings and they have access to all the human rights that any other human being should have access to. They should have access to courts. They should have access to health and all the other services of a government in the same way that local people do."

Refugee Camps Are Not Ideal

UNHCR spokesman Kris Janowski agrees that camps are not the best solution to a refugee crisis. But he says sometimes they are the only solution.

He says, "We would agree with her very much that the refugee camps are not an ideal situation. I mean, generally, the situation we have refugees . . . is not an ideal situation. In fact, it's a bad situation because people are forced to flee their own country and end up in another country, which has to host them sometimes more or less enthusiastically. So refugee camps, per se, are not ideal."

Mr. Janowski says because of security concerns, refugee camps are frequently the only remedy.

"Sometimes," he says, "they are the only possibility because the host country wants the refugees corralled in a refugee camp. They don't want them living among the population for security reasons and various other reasons. And this is primarily why we have refugee camps. It's not that we love them so much."

However, Professor Harrell-Bond says while that may be the official UNHCR position, its actions speak otherwise.

She says, "Even though the UNHCR's handbook says camps are not the best, never set up camps, unfortunately too often it's because camps make refugees visible for assistance purposes. They think it is a more efficient way to deliver health services because UNHCR doesn't have the imagination to think of other alternatives. And I think it's very seldom that governments insist on camps."

She says refugees should be allowed to "settle among the local population, seek work to support their families and therefore contribute to the local economy." She says despite the current situation, Ivory Coast has been a good example of

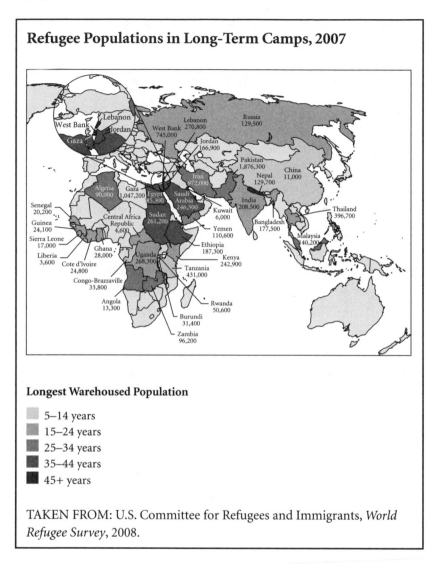

Refugee Populations in Long-Term Camps, 2007

Longest Warehoused Population

- 5–14 years
- 15–24 years
- 25–34 years
- 35–44 years
- 45+ years

TAKEN FROM: U.S. Committee for Refugees and Immigrants, *World Refugee Survey*, 2008.

this. She also says this is the case in Egypt, which does not allow refugee camps within its borders.

Integration Is a Better Option

UNHCR's Kris Janowski says, if possible, integrating the refugee population is better.

He says, "Of course, we would prefer if asylum seekers or refugees had jobs and were able to live in the community in normal housing, sending their children to schools and so on and so forth, but often it's not possible. And it's not possible because the governments that host large numbers of refugees do not want it this way."

He says refugees in camps do get some basic health care and education, but admits it is not a pleasant psychological experience. He says, however, that by and large, the refugees are safer than if they were fending for themselves.

Professor Harrell-Bond of American University in Cairo says refugee camps leave behind no benefits to the local population. She says once refugees are repatriated, the camps—some containing schools or hospitals—are destroyed.

However, she doesn't put all the blame on the UNHCR.

She says, "I think the major villain in the piece is the donors. Donors allocate money for relief programs. And that's what UNHCR and humanitarian NGOs (non-governmental organizations) feed upon. So, anything that looks like development doesn't get paid for under relief budgets. So that's the basic problem that starts it all going."

The UNHCR, like other UN agencies, is facing a budget shortfall—What it describes as "a cash flow problem that is leaving program coffers empty."

High Commissioner Ruud Lubbers says, "While needs are growing, the agency is finding it increasingly difficult to obtain the resources necessary to attend to the missions of refugees, asylum seekers and internally displaced that can be found worldwide."

It's a problem Professor Harrell-Bond says is due in part to "donor fatigue" about refugee problems.

Periodical Bibliography

Anne Applebaum — "Asylum and Hypocrisy," Slate.com, September 5, 2001.

Austin Bay — "Ending Darfur's Genocide," Townhall.com, May 17, 2004.

Eliza Ernshire — "Refugees Forever," *Counterpunch*, May 29, 2007.

Leonard S. Glickman — "HIAS Will Continue to Provide Immigration Services," *Jewish Ledger*, July 26, 2004.

Jonathan Harr — "Lives of the Saints," *The New Yorker*, January 5, 2009.

Jonathan Harr — "In Darfur, End Refugee Warehousing," *International Herald Tribune*, September 28, 2004.

Michelle Malkin — "A Reality Check for Angelina Jolie," Townhall.com, October 18, 2006.

David Martin — "The US Refugee Program in Transition," Migration Information Services, May 2005.

David Morse — "Murder from Darfur to Cairo," Salon.com, January 13, 2006.

David Morse — "Hiding the Refugee Problem Overseas," *The New York Times*, October 20, 2004.

Amitabh Pal — "What to Do About Darfur," *The Progressive*, April 18, 2006.

Philip Peters — "We Ignore Refugee Crisis at Our Peril," *Lexington Institute*, June 3, 2004.

Phillip Robertson — "Refugees the U.N. Won't See," Salon.com, January 19, 2002.

Brett D. Schaefer — "United States Peacekeeping: The U.S. Must Press for Reform," Heritage Foundation, September 18, 2008.

For Further Discussion

Chapter 1

1. After reading the viewpoints of Lavinia Limón and José Riera, do you believe that there is a serious refugee problem worldwide? Do you agree with Riera, that the boundaries between migrants and refugees are so blurred that the refugee problem is often overstated? Explain your reasoning.

2. How is climate change affecting the refugee problem? Read Teresita Perez's viewpoint on climate refugees and consider her estimate of the number of climate refugees the world can expect in the next couple of years.

3. Stephen Glain believes that Iraqi war refugees are a growing and serious problem. However, Amir Taheri disagrees, stating that information on the issue has been distorted and misinterpreted. After reading both viewpoints, do you believe that Iraqi refugees are an increasing problem?

4. Based on the viewpoints of Thomas Allen and Anna Husarka, do you believe that refugees are a true security threat to the United States? Should U.S. immigration laws be changed to be more accommodating to the victims of violence overseas?

Chapter 2

1. After reading viewpoints by David Anthony Denny and Ed Schenkenberg van Mierop, which group do you believe is best suited to tackle the worldwide refugee problem: international organizations, national governments, or non-governmental organizations? Explain your answer.

2. Ed Schenkenberg van Mierop maintains that non-governmental organizations (NGOs) are uniquely suited

to help United Nations High Commissioner for Refugees (UNHCR) in the fight to alleviate the refugee problem. After reading the viewpoint, do you agree? What do you view as the role of NGOs in the refugee issue?

3. Mauro De Lorenzo criticizes the UNHCR for having too much power and too little accountability. Do you believe the UNHCR should have that much responsibility, or do you agree with De Lorenzo that the power should be shifted to national governments?

4. What is the responsibility of the United States to Iraqi war refugees? Read the viewpoints by Brian Katulis and Peter Juul and Ellen R. Sauerbrey to formulate your answer.

Chapter 3

1. How will increasing developmental assistance help refugees in the long term? Read Merrill Smith's viewpoint to find examples.

2. Human Rights First argues that the material support bar is detrimental to alleviating the refugee problem. Paul Rosenzweig contends that the material support bar is an essential tool in the war on terror in the United States. After reading both viewpoints, with which view do you agree? Explain your reasons.

3. After reading the viewpoints by Kerry Howley, Ellen R. Sauerbrey, and Thomas Allen, how do you feel the U.S. immigration policy is working in regard to the refugee problem? Is America too lax on refugees, or does U.S. immigration policy treat refugees unfairly? Should America be accepting more or fewer refugees?

Chapter 4

1. *The Economist* cites repatriation as a useful solution to the refugee problem. The UNHCR argues that resettlement is

an excellent option when trying to alleviate the refugee problem. In another viewpoint, Sarah J. Feldman asserts that integration is an effective way to settle refugees. A final viewpoint by Barbara Harrell-Bond and Mike Kagan maintains that supporting refugee rights can help solve the refugee issue. After reading all four viewpoints, what do you perceive to be the best option? Use statistics and arguments from the viewpoints to support your answer.

2. Should refugee warehousing be eliminated, or is it a necessary evil? Read the viewpoints by Barbara Harrell-Bond and Mike Kagan and Voice of America to formulate your opinion.

Organizations to Contact

The editors have compiled the following list of organizations concerned with the issues debated in this book. The descriptions are derived from materials provided by the organizations. All have publications or information available for interested readers. The list was compiled on the date of publication of the present volume; the information provided here may change. Be aware that many organizations take several weeks or longer to respond to inquiries, so allow as much time as possible.

American Refugee Committee (ARC)
430 Oak Grove Street, Suite 204, Minneapolis, MN   55403
(612) 872-7060 • fax: (612) 607-6499
e-mail: archq@archq.com
Web site: www.arcrelief.org

The American Refugee Committee (ARC) is an international nonprofit organization that provides humanitarian assistance—such as shelter, sanitation and clean water, health care, skills training, and education—to several refugee communities around the world. Fighting gender-based violence is a focus of ARC, and the organization has developed programs to combat violence against women and girls in areas affected by armed conflict and humanitarian emergencies. ARC publishes a monthly e-newsletter called *ARC Impact*, and a variety of books, videos, toolkits, and research papers that function as valuable resources for anyone interested in the field of refugee assistance.

Federation for American Immigration Reform (FAIR)
25 Massachusetts Avenue NW, Suite 300
Washington, DC   20001
(202) 328-7004 • fax: (202) 387-3447
Web site: www.fairus.org

The Federation for American Immigration Reform (FAIR) is a national nonprofit organization that advocates for a comprehensive reform of U.S. immigration laws. FAIR works to improve border security, stop illegal immigration, protect U.S. national security, and limit the number of refugees entering the country. FAIR publishes a number of resources useful to readers, such as statistics, immigration reports, analyses on the economic and social costs of illegal immigration, and studies on the economic impact and national security implications of refugee resettlement in the United States.

Heartland Alliance for Human Needs & Human Rights
208 South LaSalle Street, Suite 1818, Chicago, IL   60604
(312) 660-1300 • fax: (312) 660-1500
Web site: www.heartlandalliance.org

Heartland Alliance for Human Needs & Human Rights is a nonprofit, independent organization that works to improve the lives of refugees, immigrants, and the poor through a variety of education, advocacy, and social programs. The organization provides legal protection for refugees; builds affordable housing; works to find affordable and comprehensive health care; and aids people to find jobs and attain economic security. The Heartland Alliance publishes a series of research reports on a number of social issues, such as human rights laws, housing and legal protections, and health care, and a quarterly newsletter, *Heartland News*.

Human Rights First
333 Seventh Avenue, 13th Floor, New York, NY   10001-5108
(212) 845-5200 • fax: (212) 845-5299
e-mail: feedback@humanrightsfirst.org
Web site: www.humanrightsfirst.org

Founded in 1978, Human Rights First is a nonprofit, nonpartisan international organization that advocates for laws and policies that advance human rights for people all over the world. One of the organization's main areas of interest is refugee protection. To that end, it has promoted legislation such as the 2008 Secure and Safe Detention and Asylum Act, which improves medical care for refugees in detention centers and provides for nationwide alternatives to refugee detention. The organization directs the Asylum Legal Representation Program, which provides free, volunteer lawyers to help refugees gain asylum the United States. Human Rights First provides an abundance of information on refugee protection and refugee detention issues, particularly resources to help refugees through the process successfully. It publishes *Rights Wire*, a monthly online newsletter, and published the 2006 report *Abandoning the Persecuted: Victims of Terrorism and Oppression Barred from Asylum.*

International Rescue Committee (IRC)

122 East Forty-Second Street, New York, NY   10168
(212) 551-3000 • fax: (212) 551-3179
Web site: www.theirc.org

The International Rescue Committee (IRC) was founded in 1933 to provide humanitarian assistance, rehabilitation, protection of human rights, economic redevelopment, and re-settlement services for people affected by armed conflict or oppression. The IRC is a global network of first responders, humanitarian relief workers, educators, health care providers, volunteers, and community activists. One of the committee's main goals is to smoothly and successfully resettle refugees in the United States. The IRC offers breaking news and eyewitness accounts of refugee crises and resettlement, in-depth information and statistics, and photographs and videos.

Refugee Council USA (RCUSA)

3211 Fourth Street NE, Washington, DC   20017-1194
(202) 541-5404 • fax: (202) 541-3468
e-mail: info@rcusa.org
Web site: www.rcusa.org

Refugee Council USA (RCUSA) is a coalition of U.S. non-governmental organizations (NGOs) focusing on issues related to refugee protection. RCUSA advocates for the rights of refugees, asylum seekers, displaced persons, victims of trafficking, and victims of torture in the United States and worldwide. RCUSA also works with national refugee resettlement and processing agencies to protect the rights of refugees and formulate policies and processes that support and improve refugee services. The RCUSA Web site is a clearinghouse for statistics regarding refugees and asylum seekers in the United States, providing reports on specific refugee issues and types of refugees.

Refugees International
2001 South Street NW, Suite 700, Washington, DC   20009
(202) 828-0110 • fax: (202) 828-0819
e-mail: ri@refintl.org
Web site: www.refintl.org

Refugees International is an advocacy organization focused on providing emergency humanitarian assistance and protection for refugees worldwide and finding a solution to the refugee problem. Refugees International also lobbies the U.S. government to condemn armed violence and oppression, and provide financial, logistical, and humanitarian support in refugee emergences all over the world. The organization issues press releases, field reports, in-depth reports, and advocacy letters. On its Web site, Refugees International has posted a variety of other resources, such as photos, videos, and a blog that offers in-depth and eyewitness accounts of refugee crises in areas such as Sudan, Sri Lanka, the Congo, and Iraq.

United Nations High Commissioner for Refugees (UNHCR)/The UN Refugee Agency
Case Postale 2500   CH-1211
   Genève de Deépôt Switzerland
+41-227398111
Web site: www.unhcr.org

Established by the United Nations on December 14, 1950, the United Nations High Commissioner for Refugees (UNHCR) was created to lead and coordinate international action to protect refugees and resolve problems relating to refugees all over the world. UNHCR strives to safeguard the rights of refugees to seek asylum and find safe refuge with the eventual aim of helping refugees return home voluntarily, integrate in local communities around their place of refuge, or resettle in a third country. UNHCR employs a staff of approximately 6,300 people in more than 110 countries to help 32.9 million persons restart their lives. The agency's Web site has a number of resources for students, including maps, posters, photo archives, leaflets, and brochures that explain how UNHCR is helping refugees worldwide. They also publish the biannual report *State of the World's Refugees*, the quarterly magazine *Refugees*, and specialized reports focusing on specific refugee crises and environmental issues.

U.S. Committee for Refugees and Immigrants (USCRI)

2231 Crystal Drive, Suite 350, Arlington, VA   22202-3711
(703) 310-1130 • fax: (703) 769-4241
e-mail: uscri@uscridc.org
Web site: www.refugees.org

The U.S. Committee for Refugees and Immigrants (USCRI) is a governmental organization that addresses the needs of refugees and immigrants in the United States by providing assistance and protection to people in need. The primary focus of the USCRI is to facilitate permanent homes for refugees or immigrants, whether that means repatriation, integration into an American community, or resettlement in a third country. USCRI directs the National Children's Center, which offers free legal and social services for unaccompanied immigrant children coming into the United States. The committee also oversees the Campaign to End Refugee Warehousing, which is a movement to eliminate refugee camps worldwide. USCRI provides a number of refugee resettlement educational materials on its Web site, and copies of the annual *World Refugee Survey* and the *Anti-Warehousing Bulletin*.

Women's Refugee Commission

122 East Forty-Second Street, New York, NY   10168
(212) 551-3115 • fax: (212) 551-3180
e-mail: info@wrcommission.org
Web site: www.womensrefugeecommission.org

The Women's Refugee Commission was established by experienced human rights workers and refugee activists to advocate
and provide resources for refugee women and children. They
focus on refugee protection, and offer a forum for refugee
women and youth to tell their stories through briefings, testimony, and international conferences. The Women's Refugee
Commission also functions as a watchdog, monitoring the
care and protection of the most vulnerable of the refugee
population by traveling to refugee camps all over the world
and offering expert assistance in a number of areas, including
health care, legal protection, resettlement services, and skill
building. In particular, the Women's Refugee Commission
provides programs in reproductive health care, detention and
asylum, and protection of youths, women, and the disabled.
The commission publishes annual reports, newsletters, and a
series of in-depth reports focusing on issues relevant to the
refugee community, such as detention and asylum fact sheets,
the situation for refugee children in Darfur, and the gender-
based violence perpetrated by young men in refugee camps.

Bibliography of Books

Alperhan Babacan and Linda Briskman, eds. *Asylum Seekers: International Perspectives on Interdiction and Deterrence.* Newcastle: Cambridge Scholars, 2008.

Erin K. Baines *Vulnerable Bodies: Gender, the UN, and the Global Refugee Crisis.* Burlington, VT: Ashgate, 2004.

Elliot R. Barkan, ed. *Immigration, Incorporation & Transnationalism.* New Brunswick: Transaction Publishers, 2007.

Michael Barnett and Martha Finnemore *Rules for the World: International Organizations in Global Politics.* Ithaca, NY: Cornell University Press, 2004.

Carol Bohmer and Amy Shuman *Rejecting Refugees: Political Asylum in the 21st Century.* London: Routledge, 2008.

Michelle Foster *International Refugee Law and Socioeconomic Rights: Refugee from Deprivation.* Cambridge: Cambridge University Press, 2007.

Jane Freedman *Gendering the International Asylum and Refugee Debate.* New York: Palgrave Macmillan, 2007.

Regina Germain *AILA's Asylum Primer: A Practical Guide to U.S. Asylum Law and Procedure.* Washington, DC: American Immigration Lawyers Association, 2003.

Jane Guskin and David L. Wilson — *The Politics of Immigration: Questions and Answers.* New York: Monthly Review Press, 2007.

Emma Haddad — *The Refugee in International Society: Between Sovereigns.* Cambridge: Cambridge University Press, 2008.

Daniel Hendrex — *A Soldier's Promise: The Heroic True Story of an American Soldier and an Iraqi Boy.* New York: Simon Spotlight Entertainment, 2006.

David Hollenbach, ed. — *Refugee Rights: Ethics, Advocacy, and Africa.* Washington, DC: Georgetown University Press, 2008.

Richard C. Jones, ed. — *Immigrants Outside Megalopolis: Ethnic Transformation in the Heartland.* Lanham, MD: Lexington Books, 2008.

Arie M. Kacowicz and Pawel Lutomski — *Population Resettlement in International Conflicts: A Comparative Study.* Lanham, MD: Lexington Books, 2007.

David Ngaruri Kenney and Philip G. Schrag — *Asylum Denied: A Refugee's Struggle for Safety in America.* Berkeley: University of California Press, 2008.

Susan Kneebone and Felicity Rawlings-Sanaei, eds. — *New Regionalism and Asylum Seekers: Challenges Ahead.* New York: Berghahn Books, 2007.

Gil Loescher, Alexander Betts, and James Milner — *UNHCR: The Politics and Practice of Refugee Protection into the 21st Century.* New York: Routledge, 2008.

Charles London   *One Day the Soldiers Came: Voices of Children in War*. New York: HarperPerennial, 2007.

Philip Marfleet   *Refugees in a Global Era*. New York: Palgrave Macmillan, 2006.

Jane McAdam, ed.   *Forced Migration, Human Rights and Security*. Oxford: Hart, 2008.

Sonia McKay, ed.   *Refugees, Recent Migrants and Employment: Challenging Barriers and Exploring Pathways*. New York: Routledge, 2009.

Sadako N. Ogata   *The Turbulent Decade: Confronting the Refugee Crisis of the 1990s*. New York: W.W. Norton, 2005.

Niklaus Steiner, Mark Gibney, and Gil Loescher, eds.   *Problems of Protection: The UNHCR, Refugees, and Human Rights*. New York: Routledge, 2003.

Kate E. Tunstall, ed.   *Displacement, Asylum, Migration: The Oxford Amnesty Lectures 2004*. New York: Oxford University Press, 2006.

Nicholas Van Hear and Christopher McDowell, eds.   *Catching Fire: Containing Forced Migration in a Volatile World*. Lanham, MD: Lexington Books, 2006.

Charles Watters   *Refugee Children: Towards the Next Horizon*. London: Routledge, 2008.

James D. White and Anthony J. Marsella, eds.   *Fear of Persecution: Global Human Rights, International Law, and Human Well Being*. Lanham, MD: Lexington Books, 2007.

David J.
Whittaker

Asylum Seekers and Refugees in the Contemporary World. London: Routledge, 2006.

Monica K.
Zimmerman, ed.

Political Refugees: Social Conditions, Health and Psychological Conditions. New York: Nova Science Publishers, 2008.

Index

A

Abdulilah, Luay, 54

Afghanistan
  human rights violations in, 71
  Northern Alliance of, 118–119
  repatriation of, 78, 93, 125–
    126, 169–171

Africa, 59, 183, 196, 198

al Qaeda (terrorist group), 52, 56,
  105, 155

Alakbarov, Urkhan (geneticist), 14

Albrecht, Thomas, 87–96

Alexander, Michael, 99

Allen, Thomas, 55–59, 131–137

AMERA-Egypt (legal aid clinic),
  195–196

Annual Tripartite Consultations
  (ATC), 175

Arakan Liberation Party (ALP),
  157

Asylum Access
  (www.rsdwatch.org), 99

Asylum seekers
  denial of requests, 43, 150–
    152, 189–190
  independent appeals for, 190
  industrialized countries data,
    28
  rejection reasons, 189–190
  restrictive assistance for, 89,
    98–99
  secret evidence against, 189
  trends in, 27–29, 105, 106
  UNHCR statistics on, 27

  See also High-Level Dialogue
    on International Migration
    and Development; Refugee
    problems; United Nations
    High Commissioner for
    Refugees

B

Bacon, Kevin, 43–44

Balkan Islands, 81, 171

Bangladesh, 33, 145

Benevolence International Foundation (BIF), 155

Biermann, Frank, 37–40

Biofuels, 34

Boas, Ingrid, 37–40

Boat movements, 28

Bolton, John, 79, 90, 100

Bosnia repatriation, 171

Brand, Rachel, 58

Brownback, Sam, 102

Bureau of Democracy, Human
  Rights and Labor, 145

Bush, George W. (administration)
  Clinton Executive Order and,
    57
  Faith Based Initiative of, 133
  human rights efforts of, 23,
    123
  Iraqi refugees and, 43–44, 49,
    50, 110
  Israeli-Palestinian relations
    and, 173
  Mexican immigration and,
    128
  "right of return" by, 173
  "War on Terror," 56, 59

C

Carteret Islands, 33
Central Africa, 81–82
Chad, 15, 16, 78–79, 124
Chertoff, Michael, 157
Children of refugees
    assistance lack of, 101–102,
    111
    education of, 125, 201
    malnutrition concerns of, 124
    material support bar and, 148,
    161
    as victims, 14, 61, 71–73, 85,
    88, 151
Chile, 175, 176
Chin National Army (CNA), 156–
157
Chin National Front (CNF), 156–
157
Chin National League for Democ-
racy (CNLD), 157
Christians/Christianity, 45, 61,
114, 150
Citizenship and Immigration Ser-
vices (USCIS), 155, 158, 160
Climate change, 19–20, 32, 34–35,
37–40
Climate refugees
    definitions flaws, 37–40
    help needed for, 33–35, 40–41
    weather-related disasters and,
    32–33
Collision Course (Graham), 132
Colombian refugees, 123, 129,
148, 150
Comprehensive Plan of Action
(CPA), 175
Conclusion of the Executive Com-
mittee of UNHCR (EXCOM),
188, 192

Congolese refugees, 181
Convention on the status of refu-
gees
    "climate refugees" under, 32
    entitlements in, 169
    integration and, 182–184
    "migrants" definition, 26
    NGO protection role, 83, 84
    "refugee" definition, 123, 182–
    183
    refugee rights and, 90, 142,
    143, 184
    refugee status determination
    procedures, 187, 191
    supervisory obligations of, 77
    travel documents and, 192
    UNHCR and, 95, 101, 145,
    169, 188
    violation of, 151
    warehousing and, 139–140,
    141
Convention Travel Document
(CTD), 192
Core Group on Resettlement, 177
Crisp, Jeff, 170
Cuban Alzados (terrorist cell),
157, 158
Cuban refugees, 67

D

Darfur, Sudan
    atrocities in, 14
    climate refugees in, 37–38
    internally displaced persons
    in, 15
    peacekeeping mission in, 16
    UNHCR aid for, 78–79
Darfur Peace Agreement (2006),
15, 16
Defense of Legitimate Rights
(CDLR), 155

Democratic Republic of Congo, 158

Denny, David Anthony, 75–79

Department of Homeland Security (DHS)
  asylum seekers and, 151–152
  defining genuine threats, 156
  immigrant visas by, 128
  protection benefits of, 154
  role of, 98–99
  screening process of, 61
  See also Material support bar

Department of International Protection (DIP), 96, 189, 190–191

Department of Justice (DOJ), 58, 77, 148, 149, 151

Desertification, 32

Development assistance for refugees
  ending warehousing, 139–140, 166
  humanitarian assistance and, 140–142
  Millennium Challenge Account, 142–143, 145
  relief-to-development gap, 140
  solutions for, 144
  in Tanzania, 145–146

Development assisted integration (DAI)
  as durable solution, 184
  local integration, 165–166
  official refugee status and, 182–184
  refugee camps vs., 181–182, 200–201

Dispossession, 45, 136

Durable solutions
  ending warehousing, 139–140
  as foreign policy tool, 62
  by NGOs, 125, 165–166
  protection rights vs., 90–91
  search for, 178
  types of, 144, 165–166, 184
  by UNHCR, 95, 110, 115
  See also Development assisted integration; Repatriation; Resettlement programs

"Duress-based exemptions," 63, 149, 151, 157–158, 160–161

E

Economic development
  armed conflicts and, 19
  global warming and, 33–34
  impact on refugees, 16, 123, 125, 141, 143, 145
  integration impact of, 166
  of Iraq, 44, 50, 52–53
  migration decisions and, 37, 182
  refugees impact on, 107, 128
  warehousing impact on, 166

The Economist, 167–173

Education programs
  for children, 125, 201
  lack of, 71
  by NGOs, 84
  in refugee camps, 72, 73, 166, 198, 201
  rights to, 184, 194
  self-sufficiency and, 125
  by UNHCR, 16

Egypt, 23, 96, 168, 200

Ethiopians, 179

European Union (EU), 29

F

"Fair and Efficient Asylum Procedures" (UNHCR), 188–189

Feldman, Sarah J., 180–184

Financial accountability of UN-HCR, 91–92

Floods/flooding, 32, 33

Forced Migration and Refugee Studies Programme, 195–196, 198

Former Soviet Union (FSU), 133

Framework Convention on Climate Change (UN), 37

Freedom of speech, 54

G

Gateway Protection Programme (U.K.), 73

Geneva Convention, 32, 101–102

Genocide, 14, 45, 82, 194

Glain, Stephen, 42–47

Glickman, Leonard, 134

Global Consultations on International Protection, 83, 177, 188

Global refugee data, 22, 23

Global warming, 19, 20, 33–35, 39

Good Humanitarian Donorship Initiative, 142

Graham, Hugh, 132

Gray, Leslie, 37–38

Green neocolonialism, 40

The Group Methodology, 178–179

Guterres, António, 69–74, 93, 169–170

H

Habibe, Rhanda, 45

Harrell-Bond, Barbara, 101, 185–196, 198–199, 201

Hebrew Immigrant Aid Society (HIAS), 133–134

High-Level Dialogue on International Migration and Development (UN), 27

Hmong combatants, 157, 161

House Foreign Affairs Committee, 105

Howley, Kerry, 127–130

Hulme, Mike, 36–41

Human rights
    Bush, George W., efforts, 23, 123
    civil liberties and, 143, 146
    Convention on the status of refugees, 90, 142, 143, 184
    durable solutions vs., 90–91
    to education programs, 184, 194
    for refugees, 194–195
    repatriation and, 71
    See also Refugee rights

Human Rights First (organization), 46, 147–152

Humanitarian assistance, 140–142

Husarska, Anna, 60–64

Hussein, Saddam, 51, 52, 54, 114

I

IDPs. See Internally displaced persons

Immigration and Customs Enforcement (ICE), 155

Immigration and Nationality Act (INA)
    material support and, 154, 156, 159, 160–161
    reforming, 64

Immigration and Naturalization Service (INS), 128

Industrial countries, resettlement programs, 176

Integrated Regional Information Network (IRIN), 56

Internally displaced persons (IDPs)
assistance for, 68
of Darfur, 15
defined, 123
in Iraq, 110–111, 115

International Catholic Migration Commission, 112

International Committee of the Red Cross (ICRC), 78, 110, 115

International community assistance, 69–74

International Council of Voluntary Agencies (ICVA), 192–193

International Federation of Red Cross (IFRC), 32

International laws for migrant protection, 29–30

International Migration and Development, 27

International Monetary Fund (IMF), 53

International Organization for Migration (IOM), 110

International Rescue Committee, 83, 124

Iran
immigration to, 50–53
Pakistani's return from, 169, 181
refugees from, 115
religious minorities in, 121
U.S. confrontation with, 44, 45

Iraq. *See* Iraqi refugees

Iraq Index (Brookings Institute), 49–50

Iraqi refugees
asylum denied by U.S., 43
civil war impact on, 61
as crisis threat, 43–46, 105, 107, 109
economic indicators and, 52–53
five measures on, 50–54
increase in, 111–112, 114
NGO assistance for, 108, 110, 112, 115
programs for, 112, 113–114, 115
repatriation of, 52, 168
U.S. help for, 46–47, 104–108, 109–115
U.S. idea of, 49–50
from War in Iraq, 20

"Iron Triangle," 132, 134

Israel, 45, 133, 172, 173

Israeli-Palestinian relations, 172–173

J

Jaburi, Ahlam Al, 43, 46

Janjawid (militia group), 14, 15

Janowski, Kris, 199, 200–201

Jewish immigrants, 133–134

Jordan, 23, 44, 45, 107, 111–114

Justice and Home Affairs Ministers (EU), 29

Juul, Peter, 104–108

K

Kagan, Michael, 99, 185–196

Karen National Liberation Army (KNLA), 58, 156–157

Karen National Union (KNU), 156–157, 159

Karen tribesmen, 58, 121, 156
Karenni National Progressive Party (KNPP), 157
Katulis, Brian, 104–108
Kayan New Land Party (KNLP), 157
Kennedy, Edward (Ted), 46, 102
Kenya, 96, 101–102, 124, 132, 145
Kenyan Refugee Consortium, 196
Kevane, Michael, 37–38
Kosovo repatriation, 171–172

L

League of Nations, 191
Lebanon, 23, 78, 112, 181, 196
Legal protections for refugees, 29–30, 190–191, 195–196
Liberia/Liberians, 78, 93, 125–126, 148, 158, 179
Lieberman, Joe, 102, 128, 130
Limón, Lavinia, 21–24
Local integration, 165–166
Lorenzo, Mauro De, 97–103
Lubbers, Ruud, 170, 201

M

Makiya, Kanan, 54
Maritime migration, 28–29
Masri, Taher, 44
Material support bar
    addressing problems with, 152
    amendments needed, 160–162
    defined, 118–119, 129, 148–149, 154, 159
    "duress-based exemptions," 63, 149, 151, 157–158, 160–161
    ransom as, 62, 63
    as tool, 58, 154–155
    wide use of, 61, 64, 156–157

Mexican immigrants, 128, 130
Migrants/migration
    asylum seeker decrease, 27–29
    international law protections, 29–30
    maritime, 28–29
    refugees vs., 26
    reversing, 47
    UNHCR data, 27
    See also Climate refugees; Refugee problems
Migration and Refugee Assistance, 112
Millennium Challenge Account (MCA), 142–143, 145, 146
Montagnard combatants, 149, 157, 161
Multilateral Framework of Understandings on Resettlement, 176, 177, 178
Mumba, Peter, 56
Myanmar refugees, 71, 129

N

Namibia, 56
Nansen, Fridtjof (Nansen Passport), 191–192
National Global Warming Community Impact Assessment, 35
National government role
    in durable solutions, 165
    UNHCR and, 90–91, 99, 101
    See also United Nations High Commissioner for Refugees; United States
National security concerns/threats
    immigration as, 56–58
    by Karen tribesmen, 58
    material support bar and, 162

Patriot Act undermined, 58–59
post 9/11, 26–27
U.S. responsibility for, 63–64
wrongful interpretation of, 61–63
See also Terrorists/terrorism
Natural disaster relocation, 32
NGOs. *See* Nongovernmental organizations
9/11 terrorist attacks. *See* September 11, 2001
Non-Albanian minorities, 172
Nongovernmental organizations (NGOs)
donors and, 201
durable solutions by, 125, 165–166
IDPs and, 115
protection training programs by, 195–196
refugee help by, 67, 68, 88, 108, 112, 124
refugee history of, 81–83
resettlement and, 175
role of, 83, 84, 85–86, 110, 166
RSD procedures and, 96, 192–193
violence against, 15–16
Norwegian Refugee Council, 40

O

Office of Internal Oversight Services (UN), 93
Oil-for-Food (UN), 53
Olmert, Ehud, 173
Oppression of people, 19, 121, 123, 148, 152

P

Pakistan, 126, 169
Palestinian refugees, 45, 113, 115, 125, 133, 172–173
Papau New Guinea evacuation, 33
"Partnership in action" (PARinAC), 82
Patriot Act (U.S.), 57–59, 61, 118, 129, 148, 159
Perez, Teresita, 31–35
Philippine's typhoon, 32
Pinochet, Augusto, 175
Plan for Global Warming Preparedness (U.S.), 35
Porter, Kenneth, 101
"Portland 7" (terrorist cell), 155
Powell, Colin, 14
Protocol for the Recognition, Protection, and Resettlement of Climate Refugees, 37–39
Public health service (U.S.), 57

R

"Reach Out Process on International Protection," 82
REAL ID Act, 61, 118, 129, 148, 159
Refugee Act (1980), 136
Refugee Affairs Division (USCIS), 158
Refugee camps
benefits of, 124–126, 132
closing down, 51
cultural aspect of, 100
in Darfur, 15
disadvantages of, 16, 70–71, 101, 199–200
diseases in, 57
education in, 72

extremism in, 169
integration vs., 181–182, 200–201
internment in, 146
long-term refugees in, 73, 103, 181
maintaining, 22
protection measures in, 81–85
refugee producing crises in, 181–182
resettlement from, 56, 101–102, 115, 165–166
self-sufficiency in, 92
standards for, 139–140
as stepping stones, 56
UNHCR involvement in, 16, 92–93, 198–199
warehousing in, 98, 102, 143, 195
"Refugee industry," 132–133, 134–135
Refugee Law Project (Kampala), 196
Refugee problems
armed conflict causes, 19
in Darfur, 15
in host countries, 126
international community assistance, 69–74
legislative support for, 149
media image of, 136
migrants vs., 25–30
resettlement programs for, 62, 113–114, 165
sexual abuse of, 124
2007 crisis, 15, 23–24
2007 refugee crisis, 15, 23–24, 43–46
worldwide, 21–24, 93
See also Asylum seekers; Children of refugees; Climate refugees; Development assis-

tance for refugees; Development assisted integration; Internally displaced persons; Iraqi refugees; Migrants/migration; Refugee camps; Terrorists/terrorism; United Nations High Commissioner for Refugees
Refugee rights
human rights for, 194–195
legal protections for, 29–30, 190–191, 195–196
UNHCR concerns over, 189–190
violation of, 186
See also Refugee status determination
Refugee status determination (RSD)
alternatives to, 191–192
for asylum seekers, 187–189
evaluating procedures for, 192–193
for protection, 94, 96
secrecy with, 190–191
Refugee Studies Center (Oxford), 101
Refugees International, 43, 105
Relief-to-development gap, 140
Religious minorities, 114
Repatriation
of Afghanistan, 78, 93, 125–126, 169–171
of Bosnia, 171
defined, 165
difficulty of, 172–173
human rights violations and, 71
ideal vs. reality of, 168–169
of Kosovo, 171–172
Palestinian refugees and, 172–173

Resettlement programs
by Core Group on Resettlement, 177
defined, 175
as durable solution, 184
functions of, 177
by Group Methodology, 178–179
in industrial countries, 176
material support bar and, 148–149
by NGOs, 175
for refugees, 62, 113–114, 165
structural use of, 177–178
by UNHCR, 174–179
by Working Group on Resettlement, 175, 177
Revolutionary Armed Forces of Colombia (FARC), 160
Rice, Condoleeza, 58, 107, 123, 156, 157, 158
Riera, José, 25–30
Rights in Exile: Janus-Faced Humanitarianism (Verdirame, Harrell-Bond), 101
Rosenzweig, Paul, 153–162
Russian Federation, 145
Ryan, Kelly, 76–78

S

Sauerbrey, Ellen R., 46, 62, 109–115, 120–126
Schenkenberg van Mierop, Ed, 80–86
Sen, Amartya, 38
September 11, 2001
immigration debate and, 118, 128–129
national security after, 26, 130

U.S. refugee admissions after, 134, 137
See also Terrorists/terrorism
Sexual abuse, 85, 88, 124
Shi'a Mahdi Army, 105
Shiite Muslims, 44, 47, 51–52, 62
Smith, Merrill, 92, 138–146
Somalia/Somalis, 56, 71, 132, 158, 179
South Africa, 56
Stern, Nicholas, 33–34
Sunni Muslims, 43, 44, 62, 105
Sweden, 107, 108
Syria, 23, 44, 45, 53, 107, 111–114, 168

T

Taheri, Amir, 48–54
Taliban government, 119, 155
Tanzania, 81–82, 101, 126, 145–146
Terrorists/terrorism
immigration impact of, 57–59, 118–119, 128–129
material support bar and, 148–149, 154
ransom demands by, 62–63
REAL ID Act and, 129
refugee risks and, 150, 151–152
See also Material support bar; September 11, 2001
Tibetan Mustangs (terrorist cell), 157
Tier I/II terrorist organization, 158, 160, 161
Tier III terrorist organization, 157–158, 161
Tuberculosis cases, 57

Turkey, 23, 45, 50, 51, 53, 114–
115, 196
Tuvalu (South Pacific island
nation), 19, 37, 39
2007 refugee crisis, 15, 23–24,
43–46

U

Uganda, 101, 175
UNAMID (AU-UN Mission in
Darfur), 16
UNHCR. *See* United Nations High
Commissioner for Refugees
United Kingdom (U.K.), 23, 40,
71, 73, 176
United Nations (UN)
 Darfur peacekeeping mission,
 16
 Framework Convention on
 Climate Change, 37
 High-Level Dialogue on Inter-
 national Migration and De-
 velopment, 27
 International Migration and
 Development dialogue, 25
 Office of Internal Oversight
 Services, 93
 Oil-for-Food, 53
 World Food Programme
 (WFP), 110, 124
United Nations High Commis-
sioner for Refugees (UNHCR)
 accountability of, 88–89, 102–
 103
 admission statistics by, 27,
 105, 106, 111, 129
 advisory role of, 76–78
 Annual Tripartite Consulta-
 tions, 175

 Conclusion of the Executive
 Committee, 188, 192
 critical aid by, 94–96, 166
 flaws of, 100
 Geneva Convention violation
 by, 101–102
 improvements needed, 92–93
 national government role and,
 90–91, 99, 101
 NGOs vs., 80–86
 protracted refugee situations,
 70–71
 reforms, 93–94
 refugee crises help by, 68
 on resettlement, 174–179
 role of, 95, 145
 shared financial accountability
 of, 91–92, 135
 as too powerful, 98–99
 Working Group on Resettlement, 175, 177
 See also Development assisted
 integration; Internally displaced persons; Refugee
 camps; Refugee problems;
 Refugee rights
United States (U.S.)
 climate refugee help from,
 34–35
 global warming and, 34–35
 Iraqi refugee help by, 46–47,
 104–108, 109–115
 Iraqi refugee idea by, 49–50
 Patriot Act, 57–59, 61, 118,
 129, 148, 159
 protection obligations of, 75–
 79, 102–103
 public health service, 57
 REAL ID Act, 61, 118, 129,
 148, 159

See also Bush, George W.;
National security concerns/
threats
United States (U.S.) immigration
policy
capping admissions, 135–137
controversy of, 134–135
education/self-sufficiency of,
125
Jewish immigrants and, 133–
134
for potential terrorists, 118,
147–152
refugee arrivals and, 121–123,
130
"refugee industry" and, 132–
133, 136
repatriation and, 125–126, 165
September 11, 2001, impact
on, 118, 128–129

V

Verdirame, Guglielmo, 101
Voice of America (VOA), 197–201

W

"War on Terror," 56, 59
Warehousing of refugees
in camps, 98, 102, 143, 195
Convention on the status of
refugees, 139–140, 141
ending, 139–140, 166
Weather-related disasters, 33
Working Group on Resettlement,
175, 177
World Bank, 53, 145
World Food Programme (WFP),
110, 124
World Refugee Survey, 21, 22–23,
200
Worst Places for Refugees list, 22

Z

Zaire, 81–82
Zambia, 56
Zimbabwe, 56